CREATING COMMERCIAL MUSIC

- Advertising
- Library Music
- TV Themes
- and More

PETER BELL

For Jackson and Conner

BERKLEE PRESS

Editor in Chief: Jonathan Feist
Senior Vice President of Online Learning and Continuing Education/CEO of Berklee Online: Debbie Cavalier
Vice President of Enrollment Marketing and Management: Mike King
Vice President of Academic Strategy: Carin Nuernberg
Editorial Assistant: Emily Jones

ISBN 978-1-5400-3004-7

Berklee Press

1140 Boylston Street
Boston, MA 02215-3693 USA
(617) 747-2146

Visit Berklee Press Online at
www.berkleepress.com

Berklee Online

Study music online at
online.berklee.edu

DISTRIBUTED BY

HAL•LEONARD®

7777 W. BLUEMOUND RD. P.O. BOX 13819
MILWAUKEE, WISCONSIN 53213

Visit Hal Leonard Online
www.halleonard.com

Berklee Press, a publishing activity of Berklee College of Music, is a not-for-profit educational publisher.
Available proceeds from the sales of our products are contributed to the scholarship funds of the college.

CONTENTS

ACKNOWLEDGMENTS

In telling the story of my experience building a successful music house, I want to acknowledge Peter Johnson, David Shapiro, Chris Rival, and Tom West for contributing their enormous talent and energy over the years to Musitech, Bell and Shapiro, and finally Bell Music. Without them there would be no story to tell.

Special thanks: Gilda Tuttlebee, David Mash, Jonathan Feist, Boriana Alexiev, John Aldrich, Connor Bell Bay, Chris Rival, Mark Walker, Katie Day, and others—as Mick Goodrick would say, "too mentionable to numerate."

INTRODUCTION

The goal of this book is to provide practical information to musicians and producers who are interested in learning to create and sell advertising music, library music, and television theme music. Certain creative, technical production, and business skills and practices are required to produce music in this space. A successful practitioner needs to know how to navigate and function in the marketplace in order to earn the opportunity to create music for profit. This book will allow you to take advantage of case studies of my work in the industry, which includes creating a long running theme for *This Old House*, as well as all types of music for broadcast advertising for many well-known commercial brands. In addition, this book serves as the textbook to my Berklee Online course, *Writing and Producing Advertising Music.*

The book covers three major categories of commercial music: made-to-order songs (traditionally and colloquially known as "jingles") and scoring for radio and TV advertising, library music, and original television theme music. Practical and aesthetic strategies and technical specifications are presented regarding what makes a great jingle or instrumental score, a great library track, or a great TV theme, so you can successfully compete for this highly sought-after work

To succeed in the field, you'll need to understand the current commercial music market: how the music is used, who buys it, and who pays for it. You must learn the various roles played in the industry and how to identify the decision makers. We'll analyze the internal organization of advertising agencies and other business entities, and describe the process of creating a bid, negotiating a budget, and communicating with clients.

This book will detail how to organize a production plan and carry out recording sessions and mix for broadcast. We'll show you how to run your business as a sole practitioner or delegate and collaborate with other musicians. We will analyze the techniques of effective advertising copywriting: writing a voiceover, lyrics, and a singable slogan known as a *tagline.*

You'll see why a commercial music composer/producer must know how to analyze, orchestrate, and arrange in familiar or unfamiliar musical genres. Finally, we'll help you master compositional and production techniques to make a musical logo memorable—with lyrics or without, in short, how to create a memorable musical hook.

I'll include anecdotes, quotes, advice, and context from my experiences working with world-class musicians and industry professionals in the fast-paced creative world of commercial music.

To access the accompanying audio and video tracks, go to www.halleonard .com/mylibrary, and enter the code found on the first page of this book. This will grant you instant access to every example. Examples with accompanying media are marked with an audio or video icon.

Many of the examples I cite in the book are protected by contract or copyright held by corporate entities. As a result, instead of actually including some of the notation, audio, or video examples, I will ask you to find them online, indicated by the following format:

For in-depth interactive study of the topics covered in this book, including embedded notation and audio or video files, video interviews, peer supported activities, discussions, graded assignments with detailed assessments, weekly online chat sessions, and more, see my Berklee Online Course: *Writing and Producing Advertising Music:* https://online.berklee.edu/courses/ writing-and-producing-advertising-music.

CHAPTER 1

What Is Commercial Music?

Music is used in virtually all productions involving electronic media. The musical score tells us how to feel and amplifies those feelings—whether we're watching a movie or listening to a radio ad, whether the musical message is manifest in lyric form, or it is just ephemeral as a barely heard underscore. From advertising campaign songs ("jingles") to corporate videos, from TV show themes to slide shows to websites, the music is vital to the message. But where does it all come from? Who decides what music to use? Who makes it? Who pays for it?

All music that is created and performed for a paying audience or recorded and offered for sale could be termed "commercial music," in a literal sense. This would include anything from a banal "on hold" instrumental phone loop to a great Beyoncé song to the immortal Beethoven's Ninth Symphony. We tend to compartmentalize music as soon as we hear it and ascribe value judgments as to the authenticity and purity of intent of the creators. We may even say, "I don't like that song, it sounds too commercial."

I believe this type of categorization is inevitable and naturally springs from our wish to aspire to high artistic values and not be manipulated by shallow faux art. I would point out, though, that judging artistic value is a pretty subjective endeavor. When I was ten or eleven years old, I fell in love with the music of Ray Charles. Later, when I heard him sing about Coke on television, I confronted a dilemma. Had he sold out? Did he really like Coke and not Pepsi? (He later sang for Pepsi!) Would he sing the same way for Dr. Pepper? I loved listening to the commercial as a piece of music; did that make me shallow or bad? What about my other heroes? James Brown, the Beatles, Muddy Waters? Once someone creates music to promote a product, are they prostituting their art forever? Or is it okay, as long as they don't allow their music to be used for ill: for cigarette ads, or for a political candidate that they despise. I think it's a good thing to confront these questions.

Is it only great music that's effective in advertising? Hardly. Sometimes, ad music is unforgettable but actually so "bad" that it's unbearably annoying. That may not mean that it's ineffective, though. In fact, we'll talk about the fact that annoying or otherwise flawed music can actually be unforgettable, just as much as an appealing hook can be. We will not often be asked to purposely create annoying music, though, except perhaps tongue-in-cheek!

Sometimes, great music flies over the head of the client. Early on, we did some demo spots for Pizza Hut featuring the crazy-good creativity of Mark Sandman (Morphine) rapping over a slow blues, among other things. We were ecstatic and thought the tracks would be a huge hit with the agency creatives, but they passed on it right away for being "too hip."

It's always interesting to have these discussions among peers. Who are our peers in this context? Other people with similar interests and aspirations are our peers, I believe, and this includes all levels of talent, skill, and experience. We're all in the same boat trying to grow as musicians. Every world-class musician has something in common with the rest of us: the fact that no matter how accomplished you are, you never "get there." Great musicians never stop learning, practicing, and growing, and they're thankful for it because it's the process that's the greatest reward. How boring would it be to say, "Okay, now I've got that music thing covered, time to take up stamp collecting." We all know that music is universal; luckily, it's also infinite.

Now that we've broadened the definition of commercial music, let's narrow it down again. We are concerned with all musical genres in our business, without exception, but we're not trying to make hit three-minute songs or three-movement symphonies, per se. We're going to make and sell music in short forms for radio and television ads, music libraries, and television shows.

COMMERCIAL MUSIC CATEGORIES

We use three categories in this book to describe primary areas of commercial music.

- jingles and scoring for advertising
- library music
- TV theme music and scoring

Other categories of commercial music may also include source music (part of the plot), game music, ring tones, music for websites, for podcasts—and more. Writing and producing for these categories can be lucrative, and the competition is fierce.

Commercial music categories are determined as a function of use, not genre or style. They have in common the attribute that the music is created with a commercial purpose in mind, beyond the considerations of an artistic or popular music career.

The music in our three main categories will either:

- promote a product, as in a broadcast TV or radio ad

- be incorporated in a Web page, video, or infomercial

- be resold, sometimes non-exclusively

- used as theme or background music for a TV show

Let's take a look at each category in more detail.

Jingles and Scoring for Advertising

This category incorporates *bespoke* (made to order) music for radio, TV, and online advertising. The music is used either to promote a product, series of products, a company, or brand. This music famously may be vocal songs with advertising lyrics (jingles), but we'll include here any custom-made music used in a broadcast advertisement, vocal, or instrumental. Historically, this music has played a huge role in broadcast TV and radio since the 1950s. With or without vocals, these tracks ideally include a musical hook built to promote an advertising slogan. We'll include underscoring here too, where the music comprises the entire audio for an ad, or scoring under dramatic action, or simply a "bed" played under an announcer performing a voiceover.

Traditionally, radio and TV spots have been 15, 30, 60, or even 90 seconds in length, but most TV ads are 30 or 15 seconds because 60 seconds or more of airtime is very expensive. This music may of course be as creative as any other musical form. Examples run the gamut, from silly and trite like "Kars4Kids" 2018, to soulful and moving like the aforementioned Ray Charles "Things Go Better with Coke" ad from 1969, or his Pepsi ads from the 1980s.

We all know many notable examples of jingles. Perhaps the most famous jingle of all time was also written for Coca-Cola, "I'd Like to Teach the World to Sing (In Perfect Harmony)," which was aired in advertisements in 1971, and subsequently became a pop hit by the New Seekers.

 "I'd Like to Teach the World to Sing"

Library Music

Music libraries are businesses that collect content for the purpose of selling or licensing it, often nonexclusively, to consumers, advertisers, video producers, and websites. Library music includes tracks sold individually or in collections for any commercial purpose. This type of music is also known as needle-drop music, stock music, or production music. It includes the industry standard five-track package: a :60, :30, :15, a full 3-minute mix, and an alternate 3-minute mix.

Prominent music libraries can be found in abundance by searching the Web using the search term "Production Music." There are lots of different rights agreements and terms available from the many music libraries in the market.

TV Theme Music

TV theme music is music that acts as an identifying theme to a TV series. It may be vocal but is often instrumental. Usually, the piece will play over the opening, the closing credits, and during the body of the program, taking the form of cues, transitions, or an underscore.

Source Music vs. Incidental Music

In addition to theme music, a show may use "diegetic" or "source" music, which is comprised of songs or instrumental tracks that are placed in film and TV as an element of the plot in a particular scene. Source music is part of the fictional setting and so, presumably, is heard by the scene's characters.

In contrast, a conventional musical television or movie score is technically termed *incidental music* and is intended to add atmosphere to the action, and to tell the listener how to feel without having a defined source from the scene or plot. That is the category into which ad scoring falls, though the term itself is almost never heard in common practice in the industry, in my experience.

Often-used subcategory terms in commercial music include but are not limited to:

- **Soundtrack.** The sound for a movie, video, infomercial, or advertisement, which may include music, effects, dialogue, voiceover, and any other audio elements.

- **Game Music.** The music and effects (soundtrack) that accompany video games. The creation of this type of music is a specialized professional category in and of itself.

- **Sound Design.** The process of creating sounds using synthesis and/or audio production techniques. Colloquially, a score that includes or features sound effects.

- **Sound Effects (SFX).** Sounds that are recorded naturally or synthesized and processed artificially, that are included in a production. SFX are ubiquitous and often important components of the soundtrack, like the famously huge sounds from the *Star Wars* movies. Many music libraries collect and resell these effects.

- **Radio ID Jingles.** A short vocal station identity song comprised of the call letters of a radio station. The FCC requires stations to broadcast an ID on the hour.

- **Promos.** Promotions for a radio or TV show.

- **PSAs.** Public service campaign spots (Public Service Announcements). An advertisement created for a charitable cause or in the public interest. The broadcaster may discount or air this type of spot for free. The agency may also donate its resources, particularly the time of its creative team. Commercial music producers also normally forgo fees for their services, although sometimes expenses are reimbursed.

- **Ringtones.** Short lo-fi samples used in cell phones to signal calls. These are sometimes a loop taken from a familiar song.

WHO USES COMMERCIAL MUSIC?

The users of commercial music are many and varied. Big corporations, ad agencies, small businesses, music libraries, television networks or local stations, and radio networks and stations all consume and may commission commercial music. As a provider of commercial music, you may consider yourself in this context as a "music house," even if you are a sole practitioner. As you supply the music, you are a vendor to the other business entities. The following is an introduction to the main players in the market who are potential clients of a music house.

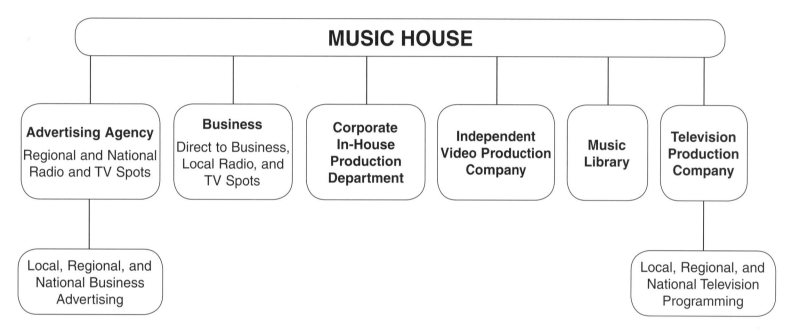

FIG. 1.1. Who Commissions Commercial Music?

Start to consider the similarities and differences in the music needs of these entities. How do they interact? Some will act as a middleman, both as your consumer and as a provider to other entities. How do considerations of size, resources, and budget affect the needs of these potential clients? How does this impact what they may or may not need from you? For instance, an ad agency may approach you with a sophisticated, fully formed idea for a campaign song. Your responsibility is to realize the vision of the agency team. On the other hand, a small business may have a limited budget, limited experience, and little or no sense of what exactly they need or can afford. You may be asked to create all the elements of the ad campaign, including a branding strategy complete with voiceover copy, lyrics, tagline, or slogan, all before you create the jingle—all of which fit the client's individual needs. We'll revisit in detail doing business with each of these categories of clients throughout the book.

Advertising Agencies

Radio and TV campaign songs (jingles) and scoring are primarily commissioned by advertising agencies on behalf of clients as part of marketing campaigns. The client hires the ad agency, which designs the ad campaign, then hires subcontractors to create the content for broadcast, then makes the radio, TV, and digital media buys. The music studio, the film production company, and the TV production studio are all vendors to the ad agencies. Part of the agencies' compensation traditionally is a markup of vendor services, including production—historically, about 15 percent, but currently, these markup fees have dropped industry-wide.

Businesses

Some businesses may run radio or TV ads without an agency as middleman. From the corner pizzeria to a local car dealer, virtually any business that promotes its products and services may potentially commission commercial music, paying for content creation and airtime directly. We'll call this "direct-to-business" work, where the music house will assume the role usually filled by the ad agency, and collaborate closely with the client to develop strategy. This additional responsibility is no small task, and requires considerable additional skill and knowledge.

Corporate Clients

Larger corporations may have in-house production departments that hire vendors to create content. They may produce corporate videos for internal consumption or point-of-purchase videos to promote products, or infomercials for broadcast.

Music Libraries

A music library may commission a composer/producer for a fee to create specific content or track packages, which they will then offer for sale.

Another common music library business model uses the practice of crowd sourcing, whereby producers upload their own tracks to a music library site that offers downloadable tracks for license. The library splits the licensing revenue with the composer/producer. Secondary clients to the music library might be any of the other users of commercial music. Video producers, corporate A/V departments, consumers, television producers, and ad agencies all use music libraries when looking for low budget alternatives to commissioning bespoke music.

Both music library models may offer a variety of deals to content providers. The resale terms may be exclusive or non-exclusive, rights-protected, or royalty-free.

Independent Television Producers and Television Networks

TV producers may commission themes and/or underscoring for shows, or scoring for infomercials or documentaries. A television station may also have a production wing. Examples include past Bell Music recurring clients WCVB-TV and WGBH-TV in Boston.

TV and Internet-based networks like Hulu, Netflix, PBS, ESPN, HBO, etc., also produce content and hire vendors for commissioned themes, scoring, and promos.

COMMON COMMERCIAL MUSIC TERMS AND TOOLS
Essential Terms

Commercial music has its own set of production-related terms and definitions that are used in communication between all participants in the process. A more complete glossary is at the end of the book, but here is an introductory list of some of the most common terms.

jingle	A song written with the express purpose of promoting a brand or product on broadcast TV, radio, Web, point-of-purchase, or any other method of publication that contains audio.
campaign song	Term of art for "jingle."
full sing	A jingle with lyrics sung throughout, often including verse, chorus, and tag. The term refers to the amount of time during the spot that features vocals, rather than whether or not there are backing vocals or harmony.
donut	A jingle with a sing at the top, then an instrumental music bed section for a voiceover, and finally a tag sing at the tail. This is a common form for a TV or radio spot. Often, the jingle will be used multiple times, with the VO (voiceover) in the middle section updated to reflect the current selling points of the client—for instance, seasonal sales or discounts.
spot	Any radio or television advertisement. Broadcasters charge a fee for each showing of a spot. The air time for a national TV and radio campaign will cost in the millions.
:15, :30, :60	Common radio or TV spot lengths, in seconds, often used to refer to a particular version of a track. For instance, an agency producer might ask, "Can you send me an instrumental mix of the :30?" (pronounced "the thirty").
music bed	An instrumental track used as background for a picture or announcement. Usually, there is minimal or understated melodic content so as not to distract from the voiceover or other audio and visual content. Also known as an "underscore" or simply "bed."
tag, tagline	A slogan, often sung or spoken at the end of a spot. In contrast, jazz musicians may refer to a tag as a quick reprise of the final cadence at the end of a song, which may be repeated. These two usages are similar but distinct.
full mix	An all-inclusive multitrack-to-stereo mixdown of any production.

alt mix	A stereo mixdown without some multitrack elements or with altered elements.
voiceover	Narrator's audio, often abbreviated as VO.
copy	Text of advertising content, especially the VO.
brand	Company or product identity.
campaign	Integrated marketing plan and strategy for promotion of a product, including branding, using all media: especially broadcast and print advertising content.
storyboard	A series of illustrations providing a representation of the finished television commercial in a sequence of scenes. Includes text descriptions and dialogue.
pitch	A sales presentation—in particular, to or by an advertising agency.
brief	An outline of the parameters of a commercial music job, furnished to the music composer/producer by the ad agency or direct client.
cut	*verb:* to edit video. *noun:* a particular edited version of a TV spot.

The Music Bed

We've defined a "music bed" as an underscore—a music track designed to be background to the spoken word or to a visual story, as in a video or film score. This may be used in a radio or TV commercial, a corporate video, a television show, a documentary, a movie—any production, with or without a voiceover or narration, or spoken dialog or sound effects. The ability to create an effective music bed is an essential skill for a commercial music producer.

An effective music bed, whether it's original music or an existing track, will have the following features:

- Appeal to the appropriate demographic.
- Fit the character of the spot.
- Match the musical pace or activity level to the intensity and style of the action.
- Establish the mood or atmosphere.
- Engage the listeners, and let them know how to feel.
- Work in the background without distracting from the message or story.
- Avoid drawing undue attention away from the VO.

Examples of beds that meet these criteria are ubiquitous in TV ads, for instance this one for GMC.

 GMC TV Commercial "Sharp"

The Brief

The commercial music producer must be able to communicate equally effectively about music with musicians and non-musicians. When a demo, jingle, score, library job, or any commercial music project is commissioned, the brief is the first line of communication. Most of the time, the brief is an email or PDF document containing a summary of the job and the information needed to complete it. This includes a time line with deadlines, financial terms, personnel and contact information, and logistical and technical submission details.

The brief will contain a detailed description of the project and the music needed, including some or all of the following:

- Type of track (song or score/TV or radio)
- Length (:15, :30, :60 or other)
- Client
- Product
- Target audience/demographic
- Voiceover copy
- Lyrics
- Tempo
- Style or genre
- Mood or atmosphere, including energy level
- Instrumentation
- Vocal gender
- Vocal timbre

The Reference Track

The brief will usually identify a *reference track*—a piece of music that has the essential qualities that the client wants for the job. The reference track is often familiar to all, such as a pop hit, standard, or a musical or movie song. If not provided, it's often useful to ask for a specific song and artist as a reference.

Most clients won't be able to describe their vision in technical musical terms. For instance, they won't say, "Make me a tune with a basic straight-eighth rock drum beat, the bass should play all roots with a constant eighth-note pulse, the verse chord progression should be diatonic I VI IV V, and use chords borrowed from minor in the bridge. Have the rhythm guitar arpeggiate the chords, also on constant eighths, and make the melody pentatonic with bluesy inflections." But they might say, for instance, "Make me a song like 'Every Breath You Take' by the Police." When you can identify a particular artist and song as a model, you have a huge head start on understanding your client's vision.

One day, a well thought out and detailed brief came into our studio. It looked something like this.

BRIEF

Demo: :30 TV   **Due:** This Friday

Title: Diet Cola: "Do Rite"

Demographic: Health and fitness-conscious domestic.
              All income. 30-50 Yrs.

Music: Medium tempo traditional blues:
          Trumpet w/mute and rhythm section
          Female vocal: Koko Taylor style
          Patterned on the classic, "Why Don't You Do Right?

VO: Salt free, sugar free, caffeine free.
       The great taste of Diet Rite Cola

Lyrics: You know the difference 'tween bad and good
           You know what shouldn't and you know what should
           Why don't you Do Rite, like some other folks do
           Why don't you Do Rite, like some other folks do
           Why don't you Do Rite

Special features: Sound FX for ballooning waist lines.

Contact: Agency: [Name]
            Copywriter: [Name]
            Art Director: [Name]
            Agency Producer: [Name]

Terms: $1,500 demo fee. $750 deposit, balance net 30 upon completion.
          Final production to be negotiated once awarded.

Delivery: Deliver online

Format: Uncompressed audio file: WAV 44.1K 24-bit

FIG. 1.2. Sample Brief

History: We knew the reference song, "Why Don't You Do Right," although I didn't know it was written by Kansas Joe McCoy. It was made famous by Peggy Lee in the 1940s. We picked Mini Gardner, a superb blues singer, whose day gig (at least, in those days) was driving a school bus. She is terrific to work with and knew the reference song. The footage shows actors drinking sugary drinks at a party and having their waistlines instantly balloon to fantastic proportions. We created a "ballooning" sound effect by me bending a string on my guitar. I did the VO myself for the demo.

 1. Do Rite :30 featuring
Mini Gardner

The Storyboard

Another tool for communication, in particular for creating music before the video for a spot is edited, is a *storyboard*—an artist's rendition of the spot in cartoon form. This is sometimes used when the agency team wants to "cut to the music" instead of having the spot edited first. This tool was developed at Disney and is sometimes used by the director shooting a spot, or even a complete movie, to plan camera angles and shots. A storyboard may contain music direction and/or cues.

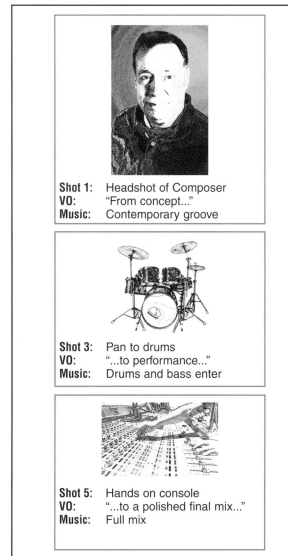

Shot 1: Headshot of Composer
VO: "From concept..."
Music: Contemporary groove

Shot 2: Pan to guitar
VO: "...to composition..."
Music: Guitar enters

Shot 3: Pan to drums
VO: "...to performance..."
Music: Drums and bass enter

Shot 4: Closeup vocalist
VO: "...to spontaneity..."
Music: Vocal scatting

Shot 5: Hands on console
VO: "...to a polished final mix..."
Music: Full mix

Shot 6: Logo
VO: "You can count on Bell Music, the home of creativity."
Music: (Full mix continues/ends)

FIG. 1.3. Storyboard for a Virtual TV :15 Spot Promoting Bell Music

ATTRIBUTES OF EFFECTIVE AD MUSIC

All effective music for advertising has some or all of the following characteristics:

- **Appropriate atmosphere.** A well-defined feeling that conveys the mood of the spot appropriate to the brand and product.

- **Accessibility.** Music that is easily understood and sung. Hip is okay; esoterically hip is not as easy a sell. ☺

- **Appeal.** The music must attract and entertain the target audience. Or annoy them; either way, it must grab their attention!

- **Identity.** The music should be in a style or genre that links the target audience to the product or brand.

- **Hook or musical logo.** Just as in pop music, the most effective musical logo is a short memorable phrase.

See if you think the Angie's List contest-winning jingle referenced below has all the attributes of effective ad music that I list above. Ben Lauenroth (who had been a student in my Berklee Online course) and I collaborated coast-to-coast to write and produce this song.

Angie's List "Rock the List"
Jingle Contest Winner

CHAPTER 2

Getting Started

In order to compete in the world of commercial music, a producer/composer/ entrepreneur needs a number of assets. These include access to studio resources, the training and talent to create professional tracks, and the ability to communicate effectively. Other important skills are organization and delegation. In order to determine what tasks we can do ourselves and what will require collaborators, we have to accurately define pertinent roles and responsibilities. Furthermore, none of these assets are enough without a coherent and effective strategy to market our services.

WHO CAN MAKE COMMERCIAL MUSIC?

Traditionally, in the days of analog tape machines and mixing consoles, a barrier to entry for producing quality music production was the high cost of music studio gear. A minimal setup typically cost many tens or even hundreds of thousands of dollars. There were some exceptions. Bonnie Raitt's first Warner Bros. album (which I'm proud to have played on) was made on a Crown 4-track tape machine set up in a makeshift studio space in a boys' camp on Lake Minnetonka, Minnesota, not a million-dollar Hollywood studio.

Now, I like to say that with contemporary technology, the means of production are owned by the proletariat. If you have a laptop, software, a MIDI controller/keyboard, an audio interface, a mic, some headphones, and audio monitors, you can make professional quality commercial music. Total cost for a great setup could be as low as five to ten thousand dollars. There are other barriers to success, but equipment costs are now not prohibitive.

FORMING YOUR BUSINESS

As mentioned, a commercial music production studio is known in the advertising world as a "music house." This term is sufficient to describe what you do, but to get started professionally, you need to choose a way to organize your business legally. Which legal business entity is right for you? Before making any significant decision such as this, you should consult a lawyer, as the laws sometimes change, and one option or the other might become a better choice for you. But as of this writing, here are my thoughts, given the current market, on how to choose the right form of business entity.

Sole Proprietorship

If you are starting your own company with limited assets, without partners or employees, and you don't feel that liability concerns will be an issue, then a sole proprietorship may be the choice for you. For example, sole proprietorships are commonly used by songwriters to establish their music publishing companies.

Partnership

If you are starting with one or more full-time collaborators, you may want to create a legal partnership. At the least, you should create a letter that discusses goals, ownership, compensation shares, intellectual property rights, and responsibilities. If signed, this will be legally binding in the case of a dispute later.

Corporation

A corporation is an ideal choice if you are starting a company that you are looking to grow in size and scope. Forming a corporation may provide protection from business-related lawsuits. In particular, an S Corporation is worth looking into. Among the advantages of this choice are some liability protections as your personal and business assets will be separated. (This does not exempt you from intellectual property liability, however!) There are legal costs to starting up a corporation, but they aren't prohibitive.

MUSIC HOUSE ROLES AND RESPONSIBILITIES

The roles and responsibilities of the participants in a commercial music studio are many and diverse. They typically fall into two main areas: business and creative production. As we list and describe them, let's be aware that in most studios, many if not all of these roles will be played, at least some of the time, by the same person or divided among a few partners and coworkers. If you are starting a jingle studio as a sole proprietorship, you don't have partners or employees, and you will need to combine all the roles into one. All of these tasks need to be done by someone, whether the business is organized as a sole proprietorship, a partnership, or a corporation.

- **Owner/Operator**
  - Acts as entrepreneur and CEO (Chief Operating Officer)
  - Maintains company vision
  - Oversees and directs all other roles

- **Producer/Creative Director**
  - Communicates with the client regarding the artistic goals of the project
  - Interprets and oversees the implementation of the client direction
  - Undertakes or oversees the composition and arranging of music projects
  - Books the talent, including composer or arranger, musicians, and vocalists/VO talent
  - Maintains a current archive of demos and contact list for all talent
  - Oversees the recording and mixing process
  - Schedules sessions and meeting deadlines
- **Engineer**
  - Records, edits, and mixes
  - Prepares projects for delivery in the appropriate format
  - Archives projects and project elements for future use
- **Business Manager**
  - Negotiates financial terms and contracts with clients
  - Keeps business and tax records
  - Invoices clients and collects fees
  - Maintains bank accounts
  - Manages loans and pays rents, outside studio fees, utilities, equipment costs, and other expenses
  - Pays employees, subcontractors, and other collaborators
  - Files union contracts
  - Maintains contracts and agreements with subcontractors, including musicians
  - Files information with performance rights associations such as BMI or ASCAP
- **Sales Director**
  - Promotes the business through advertising, cold calls, email
  - Maintains and sends out promo packages containing the reel and/or the brochure
  - Plans and implements all other marketing activities

All of these roles are in service of making music and selling it. As it happens, there is no single formula or timeline that covers all the commercial music sales and production scenarios. For jingles, scoring, or TV themes, competing for and getting the job usually comes first. Production is the second phase. Sometimes, however, production is part of getting the work, as when an ad agency holds a demo competition before awarding a job. A music library may commission a collection of tracks in a specific style or genre, but many times, tracks are created first and marketed to music libraries after the fact.

In any case, whether we have been awarded a job or we are creating tracks to sell once completed, we have to deal with the fact that no matter how talented or versatile, no individual can do everything. Your first responsibility as CEO is to assess what you can do yourself and where you'll need collaborators. You'll need to ask yourself if you can write the song. Can you write the arrangement? Can you perform the instrumental parts, the vocals? Can you read the voiceover? Can you record and mix the track?

Depending on your studio configuration, number of mics, number of inputs in your interface, etc., any contemporary full-featured DAW is capable of producing competitive, commercial music. For instrumental performance on some tracks, skillful use of MIDI and samples may suffice: drums in certain styles, or in some cases, a pop horn section, for instance. If needed, you can cover the bass part with a MIDI performance and a virtual instrument. But if you are a woman and the spec sheet calls for a male vocalist that sounds like James Brown, you must hire a collaborator. A trained musician with a powerful DAW can simulate most styles or genres, but when a high degree of authenticity is required, or you need a particular skill set—say, a bebop tenor sax part—you need to look to collaborators. Collaborators, usually paid as subcontractors, may include a composer, arranger, vocalist, instrumentalist, and voiceover artist. In addition to instrumentalists and singers, other subcontractors may also include outside service providers or vendors for such tasks as duplication, on-site recording, etc.

Some unique attributes that may be beyond your ability as an individual to provide include:

- a particular vocal range or timbre, especially if gender dependent
- a high level of familiarity with a certain style of genre
- instrumental performance skill above a certain level on a MIDI controller
- virtuoso performance on a particular instrument
- unique human sound production, such as whistling
- esoteric instruments such as washtub bass, spoons, or pennywhistle
- proficiency on any instrument that isn't easily covered by a virtual instrument
- authentic feel of a live ensemble

Experience and necessity will guide you as to which jobs need collaborators and which ones don't. It's all part of the endlessly creative and fun challenge of being an effective commercial music producer.

PRODUCTION STUDIO SETUP

The minimum entry-level equipment necessary to compete as a commercial music provider includes a full-featured project studio setup, including the following seven components:

- Computer with external drive(s)
- Software (DAW)
- MIDI controller/keyboard
- Audio interface
- Microphone(s)
- Headphones for tracking (at least two sets)
- Audio monitors for mixing

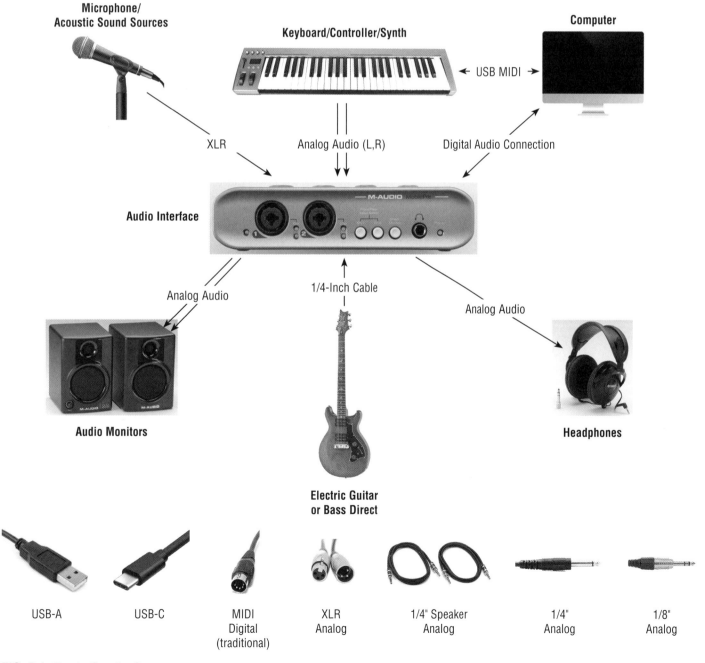

FIG. 2.1. Basic Studio Setup

YOUR IDENTITY: NAMING YOUR BUSINESS

A commercial music producer must be able to deliver music in every style and genre. We are all things to all people, but we do have a personality and an identity. Decide whether you are going to be known by your own name, the name of your studio, or a business name that says something about what you do or how you do it.

When I started out in commercial music, my then business partners (David Mash and Peter Johnson) and I thought it best to convey that we offered conventional music making, and at the same time that we were adept at contemporary technology. David Mash in fact was, and still is, a world-recognized authority on music technology. We named our company Musitech. Years later, after David Mash had left to become a vice president at Berklee College of Music, and Peter Johnson left to pursue his own music, I had a new partner, David Shapiro. We came to feel that the name Musitech wasn't easy to pronounce or remember and didn't emphasize our studio's strength as composers/producers. We were good at techie tracks, but we were even better at live ensemble music and authentic "real" music with live sessions and acoustic sound sources. Our advertising clients would tell me, "Your stuff sounds like records." We went through hundreds of name possibilities and finally chose our own names.

Our ad in *Adweek* announcing the name change read, "Throwing caution to the winds, Bell and Shapiro decide to change their name to Bell and Shapiro."

David Shapiro has since relocated to become a successful commercial music entrepreneur in New York. I'm still lucky enough to produce lots of music with David Mash, but I no longer have jingle business partners, and these days my company is named Bell Music. I'm happy with this name and don't expect to ever feel the need to change it again. The naming process can be challenging and creative. Enjoy it!

When choosing a business name, consider the following:

- **Simplicity.** The name should be fairly short. Avoid complexity. For example: Facebook.

- **Intuitive or phonetic spelling.** This will be useful to anyone searching for your name online. For example: Apple.

- **Mnemonic device.** Evoke an image or association. For example: Bell Music.

- **Acronym or initialism.** An abbreviation based on the first letters of the full name. For example: NASA (National Space and Aeronautics Administration) or IBM (International Business Machines)

- **Positive connotation.** Your name may evoke health, wealth, or wisdom, or other positive connotations. For example: Applebee's.

- **Specificity.** You may include essential information about your service in the name. For example, FreeCreditReport.com.

- **Uniqueness.** Business names are protected by intellectual property laws. You must do a search to make sure that your proposed name is not already in use. There are both free and fee-based resources for this purpose, such as Direct Incorporation and Namelab.

- **Protection.** Once you have a name picked out, you may protect it by registering it as a trademark. A free resource for trademark and other intellectual property issues is BitLaw.

Your Logo

Another way to identify yourself on any printed materials, website, or labeling is with a graphic logo.

Here's what we use at Bell Music. The concept is that the note is analog, with a hand-drawn eighth note with a certain flair in its rendering, conveying creativity. The grid is intended to convey technical proficiency. That's the idea, anyway.

FIG. 2.2. Bell Music Logo

If you know a graphic artist who'd like to help you out with a free design, you're in luck. Or if you have the resources, you can hire one. One place you can try out practicing your own logo creation skills online is www.freelogoservices.com. In addition, there are software packages available for this purpose, such as www.thelogocreator.com.

TOOLS FOR BUILDING YOUR COMMERCIAL MUSIC BUSINESS

Once you have access to studio assets that give you the ability to produce music and have organized a business model, what is the first thing you should do to try to break into the commercial music business? Identify your market. Who are the ad agencies, TV production companies, and other buyers of commercial music that you will target? And who are the providers with whom you will be in competition? The more you know about both, the better!

Start by beginning to familiarize yourself with the market participants in your area. In this digital age, you can do some of your marketing and some of your work long distance. However, you should begin in your local area because many clients and creative teams like to be physically at the sessions. For a big client, agency teams will travel, but usually only to a studio that is very well established in a major production hub, such as New York City or Los Angeles. The fact that you are nearby is an advantage when they want something done quickly and conveniently. In addition, a face-to-face meeting is the best way to start a relationship with a client. Barring that, a Skype or phone conversation is the next best thing. Mail, social media, and email are part of your arsenal, but a personal connection is the ideal.

Remember that you are not selling a commodity; you are offering to help your clients reach their goals. Always keep the clients' motivation in mind. Their agenda is to be as creative and effective as possible, and they are looking for collaborators that will help realize their vision.

Once you know how you will identify yourself and who you will try to contact, you can develop the marketing tools with which to promote your service. Take care to weigh the investment in time and money of any promotional activity, especially when you are starting out. Marketing is the tool that will help you get into a position where you can show clients what you can do for them. To succeed, you'll need to become great at composing and producing creative original music for use in a commercial production, but it's all potential until you can reach out to clients and convince them to give you a chance.

- **Social media.** Build pages on all relevant social media sites. Include easily accessible (one click) links to your reel, a brief biography, and site examples of any professional work you've done. This is the first order of business and has the advantage of being generally inexpensive or even free.

- **Mailer.** A postcard, flyer, or pamphlet can be an effective way to introduce yourself and to invite contact from potential clients. You can design and print the direct mail piece yourself, if you like. The U.S. Postal Service offers a service to create direct mail pieces online.

 USPS direct mail service

  You can develop a list of potential clients and research their addresses, or if you have the resources, you can buy a list already compiled by one of the direct marketing companies or search Wikipedia for a list of ad agencies worldwide. Sending a direct mail piece has the advantage of being tangible. The recipients will hold it in their hands, get a look at your name and logo, and can save the piece for later if they choose.

  The direct mail piece will at best be a step toward a higher goal of your marketing: the phone or in-person contact.

- **Brochure.** A brochure is higher quality and more expensive per piece to produce than the mailer, usually containing more color and photos. This approach is rare these days because of the expense and the ease of use of digital media.

- **Website.** This can be a professionally designed and hosted site, or a simple Facebook or other free page. It is a vital part of your marketing arsenal. Back in the day, the most common way to build a website was by writing HTML (**Hyper Text Markup Language**) from scratch. However, as technology has progressed, a number of far simpler and less technical options have emerged. WordPress is one such (free) option. It's an open source (meaning, the source code is freely available) option. WordPress provides a user-friendly platform that allows you to easily update your content. Another popular user-friendly option is Squarespace.

Even though WordPress is a free download, there are other costs that you will have to consider, including domain name, registration, hosting costs, the purchase of a specific theme for your site, and any design costs you might have if you are bringing in a third party to help you personalize your site. Once your site is up, you may want to look into strategies to help with SEO (search engine optimization) and if affordable SEM (search engine marketing/paid placement in search results) or PPC (pay-per-click advertising).

- **Email.** Because we all receive a lot of marketing email messages, much of it unwanted, unsolicited email messages should be brief. Keep in mind the following:
  - Be respectful. Consider your email contacts like old friends. Keep in close contact, but not close enough that you become annoying.
  - Include a call to action. Links back to your site providing additional information are great.
  - Use colored links. Keep all links blue. Studies show these are far more clickable than other colors.
  - Keep it simple. Don't make people read a lot to figure out what to do or where to go.
  - Offer free stuff. A free demo is a great way to get your foot in the door and showcase your talents. (More on this later in this chapter.)
  - Make it personal. When at all possible, try to have your email sound like you are having a direct conversation with the recipient.

Here is an example of an email that offers a call to action:

Subject: Custom music that sells

Hi,

I'm name (or I'm name, from name studio). I'd like to introduce myself as a commercial music composer and producer.

Say something brief here about your musical background and strengths.

To hear samples of my work please go to... [URL].

I'm very much looking forward to working with you and doing everything I can to help you meet your creative goals.

Please call on me to create a free demo track for your next project.

I'll do everything I can to make you glad you did.

Contact info

FIG. 2.3. Email with Call to Action

- **Cold calls.** Your strongest approach is the personal phone call. When you haven't been referred or introduced, the cold call is the classic marketing tool. This approach must be attempted with respect and sensitivity, as recipients don't want their time wasted. Be easygoing and relaxed. The best approach is simple:

  *"May I please speak to the person in charge of broadcast production? My name is [**your name**]. I'm a composer/producer looking to provide commercial music."*

  In many cases, you will be given a standard answer that might be something like the following: "Email a link to your reel to [**our address**]. It will be reviewed and kept on file by our music production department."

  If you are successful in reaching an agency producer or other creative team member, ask what they are working on. "Who are you getting your music from these days? Are you working on any jobs that need music? Do you anticipate any jobs needing music in the near future that I might be able to compete for?"

  It is human nature to emulate success. Once you have a broadcast spot or a track that clients have heard, they see you in a different light. Of course, the hard part is getting a chance to do your first job!

- **Offer a free demo.** Commercial music is a highly competitive business. Agencies often hold a competition among music providers to create original music for a spot or campaign. They provide several studios with the same brief, then collect the results and choose the track they like the best. Sometimes, the studios are in different cities. You may be competing with a studio in New York, another in Los Angeles, another in Chicago. Usually the agency will pay, at a minimum, your expenses, and often a reasonable fee above that if you are known to them as a reliable studio that will justify their investment. They won't think less of you if they choose someone else to do the final, as long as you do a good-faith job on the demo.

  Once the job is awarded, the work begins on the final music for the campaign. At this point, a full budget is negotiated according to what tracks are needed. Once you're established, you will get your chances at these competitions. The difficult part is getting an opportunity to prove yourself for the first time! The best way for a new composer to get started is to offer the agency a free demo track for any specific job the client chooses. In business, this strategy is generally known as a loss-leader. This strategy is great for corporate and direct-to-business clients as well, as long as you can realistically expect paying work to follow if your work is successful. The client has nothing to lose but the time it takes to coach you on the desired music. You should plan to do the best you can without spending a lot in fees and other expenses. One great strategy is to share the risk and reward with your collaborators. You can enlist talent to work with you *on spec* (they will get compensation if, but only if, the track sells). If you get the job, so do they.

Once you are working with a client for a common purpose, you are a partner for that project and you will build a relationship. If you do a great job, paying work will follow!

- **Follow Up.** Following up is a vital part of all your marketing activity. Leave a reasonable time between contacts. Don't "bug" your prospect.

- **Keep records.** Keep meticulous records of every call: who you spoke to and what was said. Make sure you note the time and date. The last thing you want to do is make a follow-up call too soon.

- **Evaluate the competition.** If you did get an answer to the question of who your client is working with currently, then go online and check out the persona of your competitor. Look at their graphics, the language they use to promote themselves, and their "look and feel." Listen to their demo tracks. What are they doing right? What are they doing that you think isn't effective?

- **Ask for a meeting.** Always attempt a meeting, and suggest a specific time, "Could I drop by and make a presentation? I'd like to play some of my music for you and your colleagues. I could come next Tuesday or Wednesday; would that work for you?"

If you are lucky enough to be invited to make a presentation, you'll need the most important tool of all, your demo, known by tradition in the business as your "reel."

THE REEL

A *reel*, or *demo reel*, is a collection of examples of your work. This is your most important asset when selling yourself. The name is a holdover from the days of tape, when agencies would audition your work by playing a reel-to-reel audio-tape, and/or a ¾-inch videotape. When you're starting out, you probably don't have a number of published tracks or broadcast radio or TV spots, so you must start with examples of your music, sometimes created just for the purpose of showing your potential.

You may want to emphasize a style that is your particular strength, or you may want to demonstrate diversity. A familiar issue for actors is the problem of being "typecast," where they are only considered for a certain kind of part. This happens to composers and studios as well. This can work for you or against you, so be aware of it.

The most effective reel in my experience is a three- to four-minute cross-faded composite of excerpts of your best and most relevant work. The excerpts should be short, just long enough to demonstrate mastery of a certain genre or technique (vocals, scoring, VO, sound effects, etc.). Shoot for perhaps 10 to 20 seconds per excerpt. Try to create order, transitions, and segues that are interesting and musical. Try to include as much variety as possible. Assume your listener is busy and is looking for a quick impression of your skill, creativity, and versatility.

 2. Bell Music Reel

CHAPTER 3

Production Best Practices

PRODUCING THE VOICEOVER

When you're making music, it's sometimes difficult to remember that it's being created to play a supporting role and won't always be the prime focus of the audience. For commercial music, especially in advertising, the message is the point; the music is there to help deliver the message. So, what is the focus? Many times, the message is delivered by an announcer and mixed with a music bed, hence the name "voiceover."

The VO is of vital importance to advertising, and VO artists are chosen with attention to their vocal timbre, style, and appeal. Some voiceover artists are stars in the field and can earn a high income doing this work. Usually, the client will choose the artist, or at least consult on the choice. Once you are up and running with your commercial music business, you may find that many VO artists send their marketing materials to you. You can evaluate and archive their reels and be ready to help choose the right artist for the job.

Voiceover styles have trends, not unlike any other art forms. Sometimes, a particular voice will be "Flavor of the Month" and then fade. But there are artists who endure and continue to thrive as styles change. Sometimes, an older vocal announcer style is used somewhat tongue in cheek, as with Don Pardo doing the introduction to *Saturday Night Live* for many years. An example of a terrifically successful VO artist is Don LaFontaine, a quintessential "old school" announcer. LaFontaine is nicknamed "The Voice of God" for his deep, resonant tone.

LaFontaine Geico :30

The Voiceover Session

If the clients are in physical proximity of the session, they will want to attend the voiceover session, give direction, and have the final say on the performance. Often, the direction will have to do with the level of energy of the VO, or the feel of the spot. The artist might be asked to do an aggressive "hard sell," or alternatively told to underplay the copy until the tagline or call to action, or go for a subtle or low key approach. The client may also want some of the copy to be performed with added emphasis. This is usually a smooth and welcome collaboration, but in some cases, it can be a difficult experience.

"Blooper's Soap" is the work of some VO actors and producers who decided to spoof the process. This hilarious parody was written by Daws Butler, the voice of many of the Hanna-Barbera cartoon characters, including Yogi Bear. It was made in the late '50s but still resonates today. Remember, if this happens to you, the client is always right. ☺

Daws Butler Blooper's Soap

Another example of parody is a VO that was improvised by actor, musician, and VO artist Tim Jackson during a session we were doing for a company selling a Romanian cream that claimed to reverse the aging process (since discredited).

3. Tim Aging

The Voiceover Artist's Skill

Aside from the acting ability of the VO artist, there are a number of technical skills that are in demand. The VO must be easily understandable, crystal clear, and deliver a lot of information in a short time. Copywriters don't get paid by the word, but you wouldn't know it by their work, usually. Often, the issue is one of how to fit everything into the allotted space. In the old days, before digital editing, the artist who could speak intelligibly at a fast clip would always be in demand.

The most well-known practitioner of the speedy VO is John Moschitta, Jr., who was so fast that his skill became the focus in a series of ads for Federal Express and other companies. As you listen to this ad (among the most award-winning ads of all time), keep in mind that this was produced in 1981, still the era of tape-based recording when you couldn't speed up audio without changing the pitch and timbre and hearing the "chipmunk effect."

In his famous FedEx spot, John Moschitta, Jr. speaks at a rate similar to his Guinness Book of World Records mark of 586 words per minute. Keep in mind that in this case, Moschitta is not doing a voiceover per se, as he is an on-camera actor performing dialog. The VO is done by another artist reading the tagline at the end, "Federal Express, when it absolutely, positively has to be there overnight."

FedEx Moschitta Speed Read

Since contemporary processing can easily accomplish time stretching of audio, now everyone can be more like Mr. Moschitta. Melodyne is a software pioneer in this space. All professional level DAWs currently have a built-in time stretching capability as well. As usual, moderation is the key to effectiveness with this process, or as with Moschitta's FedEx spot, the effect itself becomes the message, rather than the intent of the ad copy.

Keep in mind that an accomplished professional VO artist can look over the copy for a short time, take direction, and often read it perfectly in the first take, with great pacing, dynamics, vocal timbre, and mic technique—as Chris Rival says, "like a great singer." That said, sometimes production techniques will be necessary to create an optimized read.

VO Production Techniques

There are a number of production techniques regarding voiceover recording and editing that a commercial music producer would do well to master.

Composite Editing

The most important of these is composite editing, or "comping." The producer chooses the best parts of multiple takes and edits them together for a final seamless performance, called a "composite track" or "comp." If necessary, in order to avoid clicks and pops that arise from appending regions, overlapping, or butt splicing, the segments may be faded or crossfaded.

Contemporary DAWs streamline the process by the built-in "comping" features. The takes are recorded on top of each other on the same track in lanes. Then the producer simply uses selection to audition phrases or segments, and chooses the best for the composite track, whether it be a guitar lick, a vocalist's phrase, or a VO artist's line, or even a single word. Of course, this is a great method to remove breaths as well, if desired.

Usually, the client will attend the voiceover session and make decisions regarding the preferred phrases from the various takes to include in the final comp. In the case of ad agency work, the creative team usually has a lot of experience to draw on, and they know in detail what they want. Remember, the aesthetics of the voiceover are as important as the music.

Editing a Voiceover to Fit

Once you have a clean performance, you still have to fine-tune it to fit the time constraint of your spot length. You will find that in most cases, you'll be trying to fit too many words into your spot.

Quickly and roughly line up the VO region to the bed, and cut between phrases. Trim the beginnings and endings of regions so that there is no lag time or empty space, but no audio is clipped off. Shift the regions to fit, keeping in mind that you want the transitions between phrases to sound natural. Finally, audition the completed edit to make sure no words are clipped or lost and that the timing works. Compare the example of a "raw" unedited VO to the edited version in this pair of audio tracks.

4. VO Raw
5. VO Edited

Choosing the Microphone

A great place to research mics is on the online music store sites. They will have lots of technical info, prices, and reviews.

There are certain mics that are preferred for voiceover work—for instance the Neumann TLM 103 or the Electro-Voice RE20, which is the industry standard for broadcast. These mics are effective at dealing with the *proximity effect*—an increase in the lower frequencies as the sound source moves closer to the mic.

FIG. 3.1. Electro-Voice RE20 Microphone. This is the classic dynamic cardioid microphone favored by announcers since its release in 1967, designed successfully to counteract the bass-boosting proximity effect.

Processing Tools

There are a set of processing tools that producers use when recording and mixing voiceovers that are standard in the industry. In the old days, there were stand-alone external hardware devices to accomplish each task, but in the modern recording environment, EQ, the de-esser, compression, and side-chain compression are available in software. If you aren't happy with the functionality that comes with your particular DAW, these tools are available as third-party plug-ins from Waves, iZotope, and other companies that specialize in production tools.

- **De-Esser.** In addition to using a pop-screen during recording, which attenuates *plosives* (the distracting lip transients often heard with words that start with a hard consonant), the industry standard for voiceovers includes the use of a de-esser, either as a stand-alone piece of gear or more often now as a DAW plug-in. The de-esser is a dedicated form of compression used to attenuate excess sibilant consonants. Aside from this automated approach, some producers will use volume automation to reduce individual instances of unwanted sibilance by creating a short level notch at the offending sound. The audio tracks show how a de-esser can isolate and attenuate sibilance.

6. VO with Sibilance, No De-Esser
7. VO with Sibilance Isolated by De-Esser
8. VO with Sibilance Attenuated by De-Esser

- **EQ.** On voiceovers, it's standard to use a high-pass filter at 80 Hz for males and 130 Hz for females to increase clarity and avoid low-end muddiness. Other adjustments are made to taste, and sometimes, a radical effect is requested to create a dramatic effect. Most DAWs have many such options built-in as presets, like Logic's Phone Filter Notch EQ setting, which distresses the signal in a way similar to a vintage telephone connection.

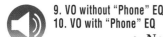
9. VO without "Phone" EQ
10. VO with "Phone" EQ

- **Noise Gate.** Another good tool is the noise gate, which can eliminate low-level noise between phrases. It allows the signal to pass through if it is above a certain threshold. It does not remove noise from the signal, so always take care to record with a high signal-to-noise ratio even if you plan to use the gate. Also, make sure to use hysteresis, if it's an available parameter, to make sure you don't clip off the end of words or phrases. Another efficient way to accomplish this in a DAW is to use a region editing command that snips out areas below a set threshold ("Strip Silence"). Keep in mind that there are cases in which continuous live ambient sound is desirable, so invoking any of these strategies would not be appropriate.

- **Compressor.** Compression is used either on the way in, during recording if you have an outboard compressor or DSP (Digital Signal Processing) in your audio interface, and/or after the fact during processing in your DAW.

  Compression attenuates peaks in the signal that exceed a threshold, thereby reducing the dynamic range. Once the peaks are controlled, the entire VO signal level can be raised without causing clipping. The result is that the quieter parts are now louder. This tool can really help to increase the clarity and presence of a voiceover, but if overused, it can cause the vocal to sound "squashed." For that reason, sometimes using volume automation for problem spots is a good idea. The broadcast media have their own compression that they use on all their audio. In the case of radio, the compression is pronounced already, so extreme compression when mixing a radio spot may result in an overly saturated track once broadcast.

11. VO with No Compression
12. VO with Compression

- **Ducking, with Side-Chain Compression.** Side-chain compression is sometimes used to automate the process of ducking the music bed when the announcer is delivering the VO copy. In the spaces between VO segments (if there are any), the bed automatically is mixed louder, but is lowered under the spoken segments. In a compressor plug-in, for instance, you can select a track to assign to the side chain. The compressor will add the chosen signal (the "key") to the input of the compressor, which will then attenuate the music output according to the strength of the incoming signal. This can be tricky to use effectively as the compressor may audibly pump in a distracting manner, so if you try it, use moderation.

VOCAL CASTING AND ARRANGING CONSIDERATIONS FOR JINGLE PRODUCTION

Choosing the vocalist for a song is as important as any single decision you make as a producer. Considerations include style, age, gender, timbre, and range. It's fine to create your song with a generic sounding voice. In fact, in the old days, the agencies preferred generic voices, as they were very risk averse. The standard sound was a middle-of-the-road voice that wouldn't ruffle any feathers, harmonized with a small group or even a big chorus. This is not to say it wasn't good music; it was just safe. A good example is the Chevy campaign of the early fifties, "See the USA in Your Chevrolet," performed by Dinah Shore. Fifty years later, Chevy aired the same song produced with the cast of *Glee*. This time, not so tame! The style of music in advertising changed forever with the advent of the Ray Charles, Aretha Franklin, and Michael Jackson songs for Coke and Pepsi. You still hear a lot of "generic" knockoffs of a current style that sounds far from genuine, but nowadays, all styles of music are used in advertising, and in many cases, the more genuine the performance, the better. Since the 1990s, the ad agencies have been licensing pop hits for their spots instead of having original songs created, as evidenced by this brilliant 2010 spot for Kia featuring the Black Sheep.

Kia ad, "The Choice Is Yours"
Black Sheep

Of course, we don't often, if ever, have a budget that will support the hiring of a superstar, or a Broadway cast. Can you imagine what it cost to produce the Chevy/*Glee* piece? However, we can adapt to the fact that these developments have opened up the ad world to a level of authenticity that it wasn't comfortable with in olden times. Sometimes, you'll still get a client that wants a generic sound, and there's nothing wrong with providing that. However, my recommendation is to choose a vocalist who specializes in the style you are working with. If it's reggae, hire a vocalist who grew up singing reggae. If it's jazz, hire a jazz singer, etc. This is not always possible, so you do the best you can. A good jingle singer can imitate any style, and some are brilliant mimics. To paraphrase the Coke ad, there is nothing like the real thing, but if that isn't available, we'll get as close as we can get.

Vocal Range

Most jingles are pitched so that an average voice can sing along with them, for obvious reasons. Keep in mind the dynamic level of the song. A singer's quiet range will be different than their belting range. They will have an upper limit to the chest voice, and then another higher upper limit to the falsetto/head voice.

A place to start for a vocal range for a female is G below middle C to C third space on the treble clef, and for a male, the F an octave and a fifth below middle C to F above middle C. Every vocalist is different, of course. Some of the greatest singers of all time have or had a limited range—for instance, Billie Holiday.

FIG. 3.2. Vocal Ranges, Female and Male

How to Paint Yourself into a Corner... and How Not To

Once you have chosen your vocalist, make sure not to make assumptions about their natural range. You can ask the vocalist, ahead of time; they will know their range. Or, you can simply play or sing your melody to the vocalist, even over the phone if more convenient, making sure to include the lowest and highest notes. They will know if it's comfortable right away and let you know how to adjust. Pick a key that works, and transpose your song. If your track resides in mostly or all MIDI form, this is pretty simple to do. If you plan to have an elaborate arrangement with a lot of acoustic sound sources, then find the singer and learn their range before you produce, or risk a disastrous waste of time, energy, and money.

I made this mistake once when I forgot to check my melody ahead of time with the great singer/songwriter Jonathan Edwards before he came to the studio to sing a jingle for us. I arranged the track in a key that took the melody range too high. He was only in town for a short time for a concert, so I didn't have time to transpose the song and produce a new track for him. He has a beautiful high tenor voice, and he was able to hit the notes, but I learned my lesson.

Vocal Arranging as a Collaboration

Vocal arranging is a specialty. Not all of us are adept at singing or arranging vocals. If that is your talent, by all means, do it yourself. However, there is nothing wrong with relying on your ability to judge singing talent in others as you put together the right team in an effort to create great vocal performances and arrangements.

Once you have the key, you can almost always rely on your vocalist for creative collaboration. In fact, most vocalists are adept at overdubbing harmonies to their own lead tracks.

In many cases, you won't even have to try to work out harmonies yourself. Your vocalists can improvise them on the spot. An example of what happens when you put four or five extremely talented singers in a room and let them improvise is a gospel version of "My Blue Heaven" that we covered for Labatt's. We created a completely improvised rendition of the classic song, timed to fit the spot. We chose guys we knew could sing gospel: Armsted Christian, John Warner, Joel Hiller, Rodney Young, and Ray Greene, and then turned them loose.

13. Labatt's Gospel :30

In the case of spots we produced for Freihofer's Baking Company, we were lucky enough to be able to work with accomplished songwriter and vocal arranger Jack Perricone, past chair of the Songwriting Department at Berklee. This time there was no improvisation. He composed and arranged a series of jingles for us that were broadcast as part of a TV and radio campaign for this national baking company based in upstate New York. He wrote everything out in standard music notation and chose his own vocalists, the brilliant group Vox One, featuring Paula Cole, Paul Pampinella, Yumiko Matsuoka, Tom Baskett, who he knew had the skills necessary to read and perform his arrangement.

14. Freihofer's Cupcakes :60

PLANNING AND PRODUCING
A LIVE RECORDING SESSION

A modern producer has many options for how to create a track. There is a continuum of choices available, starting with a track created entirely from samples and virtual instruments, and ending with a track that is entirely comprised of acoustic sound sources. Let's consider some of the criteria for determining what kind of track to create.

Schedule

Sometimes, your client may want a demo or even a final track done so quickly that planning, scheduling, and carrying out a live session is impossible. First, the client must approve the schedule, and they will probably want to attend the session. Then, you'll need to choose the appropriate talent and check their availability. There may be multiple sessions involved: the basics, horns, solos and sweetening, vocals, and background vocals. All this can take anywhere from three to ten working days.

If you need to deliver a song tomorrow, it's a different story. So, you crank up your DAW, create a track, add whatever live elements you have time for, add vocals, and mix. This time pressure is part of the job. It can be exciting, pushing you to do some of your best work.

Access to Specific Talent

Whether to compose and arrange a track by doing everything myself can be a decision forced by schedule or budget. But if time and resources allow, my preference is to involve the right player for the right job. I've made the mistake of booking a great jazz drummer on a funk track and having the result be so inappropriate that we felt that we had to do the session over. Players, vocalists, and arrangers can be versatile, but there's nothing like booking someone for whom the style of the piece is second nature. You may be a great guitarist but not play slide. If you do play slide, you could be great at playing country lap steel, or Hawaiian steel, but not Delta blues or rock slide guitar. When in doubt, and if you have time, a great way to know for sure is to go out and hear the player in live performance.

Word of mouth and your own experience are key to this process. You will build a network of contacts among musicians that will usually be accurate in recommending the right player, the right arranger, and the right session leader for the job. When resources allow, it makes sense to use specialists to arrange the various sections. Often, the best vocal arrangers are vocalists, the best horn arrangers are horn players, etc.

Budget

If you are working with a budget for a small business or video producer, or creating a library track, you may do the entire track using modern DAW technology. You can add live elements as your resources allow.

If you are working on a demo for a specific job, you can sometimes hire talent "on spec." Be sure to make the terms clear ahead of time. For instance, you could say something like, "I'd like to offer you one three-hour 'on-spec' demo session with no guarantee of payment unless I make the sale. If the demo is successful and I get paying work from it, then your fee will be $300, with an additional $200 if there is a call-back session. I will pay you as soon as my client pays me." Dollar figures mentioned are, of course, for reference only and will vary according to local market conditions and individual musicians.

Another possible cost-cutting approach is to use the concept of economies of scale. It may be possible to do more than one arrangement or track in one session, as long as you are careful not to mislead your client about your process. This isn't always practical, but in the case where it does work out, you will see significant savings, as you are paying by the session, and charging by the track. In the case of subsequent work, especially for agencies, they may have budgeted for a full session for each arrangement, and fully expect the invoice to reflect that.

In general, a full live session is regarded as value added, and the budget will reflect that. For instance, if a song calls for two guitars, bass, drums, keys, horns, lead vocal, and background vocals, it can add up, but the cost may be relatively small to an advertiser who is spending hundreds of thousands or millions on media buys. Whether you are working with a budget of $500 or $15,000, it's usually a good idea to include as many live elements in the track as is practical.

Access to Appropriate Studio Space and Assets

When I'm planning a job, my first decision is whether or not to include live drums. I have a nice project studio at home where I can make professional tracks with some high-end gear, a professionally wired patch bay, and professionally built sound booth. I can record acoustic instruments, overdubbing usually one or two at a time, and vocals or horns up to a group of three, but I don't have enough room in the recording booth to record live drums. Therefore, I sometimes use other studios. But this is my home studio, which serves me well for many kinds of projects.

Peter Bell's Studio

Computer - iMac Pro
- 3.2 GHz Intel Xeon W
- 32 GB RAM
- 1 Internal 2 TB SSD Drive

Storage
- 2 External 2 TB Drives
- 4 External WD Passport 1 TB drives
- 2 External 1 TB drives
- 4 External 500 GB drives
- 2 External 650 GB drives

Displays
- Apple LED 27-inch Cinema Thunderbolt display
- Built-in 27-inch retina display (iMac Pro)

Music Production Software
- Logic
- Pro Tools
- Reason
- Sibelius
- Audacity
- iZotope RX
- iZotope Ozone
- Waves Diamond Bundle
- Universal Audio: Full Suite
- Ivory
- NI Komplete Ultimate
- DrumCore4
- Melodyne
- Omnisphere
- Trillian
- Hive

Audio Monitors
- Genelec 1031A Studio Monitors
- Yamaha NS10 Studio Monitors
- Realistic Minimus-7 Monitors

Headphones
- Audio-Technica ATH-M40fs Headphones (6)
- AKG K712 Open Back Reference
- AKG 553 MKII Closed Back Studio

Audio Interfaces
- Universal Audio Apollo Quad w/Thunderbolt 3
- Presonus AudioBox iTwo

MIDI Controllers
- M-Audio Keystation Pro 88 controller
- M-Audio Oxygen 25
- Korg Nano Key

MIDI Interface
- Emagic Unitor 8 MIDI interface

Microphones
- Electro-Voice RE20
- Beyerdynamic MC 740N (C) P48
- Shure KSM 44
- Shure SM58

Other Studio Gear
- Samson Servo 200 power amplifier
- 96 Point TT cable patch bay
- PreSonus HP60 6-channel headphone amp
- PreSonus HP4 headphone amp
- Korg DT-1Pro rack-mounted tuner

Guitars/Basses
- Fender Stratocaster
- Dana Bourgeois acoustic
- Guild D 40 acoustic
- DeArmond X-155 hollow body
- Music Man Sterling bass: active pickups
- Fender Musicmaster bass: passive pickups
- Various guitar and bass amps

FIG. 3.3. Gear in Author Peter Bell's Studio

Workflow Issues

There are workflow issues stemming from the fact that the studio is in my house.

1. In traditional studio design, the producer/engineer looks straight ahead through a double glass window into the booth. I have to crane my neck for a limited view through the double glass doors.

2. The size of my sound booth is limiting, although it is fine for VO, vocals, soloists, guitar amp, etc. It's too small to be a full drum room or to record ensemble groups such as a full horn section.

3. I have forced hot air heat and central air conditioning in my house. Even though my booth has extensive sound insulation and treatment installed by an experienced studio designer/builder, both heat and air are noisy and have to be turned off during recording of anything acoustic, vocals, etc. I also turn off the refrigerator because it generates a low hum, and of course nobody can take a shower, or use the washer/dryer upstairs during recording. ☺

If the job calls for live drums, I go to an outside studio. Here are some additional requirements for various types of recording.

Live Drums

To record live drums, you need:

- A room large enough and sufficient inputs in your audio interface to record the required ensemble.

- Mics appropriate to the task. A drum kit typically is recorded using at least four to six mics. Kick and snare are almost always mic'd individually, hats and toms sometimes, and two mics are standard for a stereo overhead sound.

There is lots of readily available advice online on miking drums.

 **Drum Mic Placement Shure (for instance)**

Vocals

Background vocals require optimally one mic per vocalist for a group of four or less. This gives you the most flexibility for processing and levels in the mix. Alternatively a single mic set to a bidirectional (figure-8) polar pattern is often used. If, and only if, the singers are experienced enough, they can face each other and match each other's timing and create a blend by ear, saving mixing time.

Horns

Horns usually require one mic per horn for a group of four (or less), for the same reason.

THE LIVE RECORDING PROCESS

Unless you have a soundstage-sized recording facility, you may have to do multiple sessions to cover all the parts. Even if space is not a consideration, if you have sufficient time, it's a good idea to divide your planning into individual sessions, as described below.

The recording process is usually broken up into separate sessions:

- **Basics.** Rhythm section: drums, bass, guitar, keyboard. If possible, it's a good idea to put down a reference vocal when doing basics so the musicians can respond to the singer. Sometimes, you may even get a final vocal out of the session if you're lucky.

- **Horns.** Three, four, or six horn parts are most common.

- **Strings.** Solo or group live strings are a wonderful value added to a commercial music track.

- **Solos.** Often, the solos will be overdubbed, especially if the player is a member of one of the other sections.

- **Vocals.** Lead and background vocals. The classic grouping is three, but four or six background singers are also used. The client will usually want to attend, and have input, into the vocals session.

- **Sweetening.** Any session devoted to overdubs or embellishments may be referred to as "sweetening."

Preparation

Song session players and vocalists are used to taking part in the creative process. They will be glad to improvise or help arrange and compose collaboratively on the spot. That said, I can't stress enough how important it is to be prepared. Different contributors will need and expect different assets to be given them before and during the session.

Vocalists will need lyric sheets, preferably printed in large type. It's better to print them than to have them use their phones so they can make notes on the page during the session. They will also need to learn the melody and the backup parts efficiently. You can handle this best by sending material ahead of time. An MP3 with a scratch track and scratch vocal is most common. For vocalists that have music theory training, you can write the melody or parts out, but this is usually not necessary for vocals. If you're not able to sing a scratch vocal in the correct key, you can play the melody in with a guitar or keyboard. Once the vocalists have learned the song, you can let them interpret and expand on the melody. Sometimes, they will exponentially improve your initial melodic ideas.

When doing background vocals, choose one vocalist to lead/conduct. Position singers so that they can see each other's faces. Sometimes, for words that start with T or S, assign that sound to a single vocalist and have the others sing the word without the first letter, to avoid cascading consonants.

Rhythm section players will be fine with a chord chart or lead sheet and specific style direction. Absent a written chart, if the arrangement is simple enough, it can even be talked through. This is usually known as a "head chart," as there is no written music.

There are a couple of standard ways to prepare the written chart, if one is used. It's common to use shorthand techniques, such as writing out the important melodic parts, providing chord symbols, and slash-mark rhythms, and simply note the form below as a list of rehearsal marks.

Another approach is to use Arabic or Roman numerals, so the players can instantly use their knowledge of scales and diatonic chords to transpose easily if necessary. Sometimes, this type of chart is referred to as a "Nashville Chart," because it is common in Nashville studios where players are often changing keys on the same chart for different vocalists.

Horn players and string players will expect the parts completely written out, usually in Sibelius or Finale, but a handwritten part is fine as long as it's legible. Remember, you are paying the players for their time as well as their talent, so don't make it harder for them to read the parts than it needs to be. Good horn or string players will not need the parts ahead of time; a couple of times through the chart, and they will have it. If music notation is not your forte, it shouldn't hold you back at all, as you can certainly work with an arranger either by playing or singing ideas back and forth, or by preparing scratch tracks of the parts as MIDI performances in your DAW.

Vocalists are usually aware of their range, so as noted before, it's a good practice to work with them on this issue ahead of time before committing the project to a key. Of course, with DAW technology, it's possible in some cases to use processing to transpose the elements of an audio track, but it's always better to get it right the first time.

Whether it be written parts, scratch tracks, or lead sheets, the key to a good session is preparation. Remember, the talent will share their creativity but rely on you to make final decisions in all cases. The more time you spend preparing with your client, and on your own, the more you will be ready to communicate your vision for the project, and the better chance you will have of realizing it.

Hosting Clients at the Session

What will help you compete and win when the clients are attending your sessions? When you start out, you may not be able to afford a fancy recording studio with a luxurious client area in your control room with refreshments and catering, but even in the early stages, you can try to create a comfortable environment where your agency team can feel involved and productive.

It's important to have room for clients as they observe and make decisions during the production process. When you're getting started, this space may be your living room or whatever space constitutes your home studio. Try making it as comfortable as possible.

Make sure you have a large display for screening video. It's not ideal if three people have to look over your shoulder at a two-inch video streaming on a laptop. If possible, provide a display that's large enough so that the team can easily see it as they take part in the creative process.

A little bit can go a long way in making the agency team feel at home. You'll save them time and effort if you offer coffee, soda, or send out for lunch. You'll make these expenses back many times over if you get repeat work from the agency. When Bell Music started getting agency work, we were able to open a client-friendly state-of-the-art studio on Newbury Street in Boston, within a short walk or ride from the Boston ad agencies.

The agency creatives will want to provide direction to the talent directly, especially in the case of voiceovers. You can inexpensively provide direct talk-back access to a client by using a headphone amplifier that has that feature built-in, with an external XLR mic input. I have mine set up so that the client can press a foot switch to activate a room mic when giving direction to the talent in the booth.

If you are working from a home studio and don't currently have a fancy studio space, do the best you can. Good agency teams are more interested in talent than appearances. When a larger space is needed, simply incorporate the added cost into the budget and go to a bigger studio.

MIXING AND MASTERING AUDIO FOR BROADCAST

Mixing music is a vast area of expertise that we spend as much time trying to master as we do music itself.

Let's first quickly review some basic concepts regarding mixing. To make a good stereo mix, you must work with balancing various sound sources. You'll work with:

- **amplitude:** balancing levels
- **panning:** spatial placement in the stereo field
- **spectrum:** equalization tools for affecting the tone
- **dynamics:** compression and limiting for controlling dynamic range
- **reverb:** enhancing the sound while creating a sense of dimension
- **other time-based processing:** delay, flanging, echo, chorus, amp simulation, etc.

There are some issues to keep in mind when mixing any kind of music. A great mix is never done, but you reach a point when you have to move on with your life. Our ears get tired, so take frequent breaks when mixing. When you get a chance, let a mix go overnight and listen to it after a good night's sleep.

When mixing for advertising, keep the focus on the vocals and the VO. The music is there to support the message.

When you mix a VO, make sure that unless it's a special effect like a flashback or a dream, you will never use reverb on the voiceover. A dry VO will bring the message closer and give it a more intimate presence. Mix or check your mix on audio monitors if possible, rather than only in headphones. Headphones sound brighter than speakers because we "hear" lower frequencies with our bodies as well as our ears, and with headphones the sound is isolated to our ears. We need to mix so that the track sounds as good as possible on most playback systems.

In the commercial music and song world, we work with deadlines. You may only have a fraction of the time you normally take for a mix that you might create for personal artistic purposes. Plan ahead for this, and do the best you can in the time allotted.

Involve the ears of other people, if you can. You may be reticent to mix with your client there, but it's actually a great idea so that you can avoid having your work returned to you for a remix. You are always balancing your own musical aesthetic sense with the requirements of making an effective ad—the main agenda of your client. If your client says that the voiceover isn't loud enough, you should adjust the balance, even if it drowns out the most beautiful musical moment in the piece. If you don't, you won't get repeat work.

Advertising tracks are ultimately played on low fidelity systems, for the most part. Your track will probably never again be played on high-quality audio monitors after it leaves your studio. It will be heard on tiny computer speakers, mobile device earbuds, car speakers, or TV speakers. For this reason, it is vital that you mix, or check your mix, on small, inexpensive speakers. Listen on your laptop. Put it on your phone, and use Bluetooth to listen in the car. Make sure you have lo-fi monitors you can use in the studio. It does the product being advertised no good if the mix sounds great on your expensive Genelecs but the bass is inaudible on the end-user's iPhone.

Mix "in the box" using your DAW, and use automation as much as you can. In the pop world, once a mix is done, it is published, and that's the last time you'll mix it. In the commercial music world, you are constantly remixing with a new voiceover, or a new lyric performance, or a newly configured form. You will save yourself countless hours if you save your mix and archive it.

Mastering and Delivery

Mastering a song is the art of fine-tuning the finished mix by using EQ and compression and other processors on the finished stereo mix to maximize the sound quality for the intended use. Mastering is a specialty, done by dedicated engineers in studios designed and equipped for the process. In ad music, however, mastering is done in-house by adding processing to the output channel strip as part of bouncing the final mix.

Compression and the Loudness Wars

Radio and TV stations compress all the audio material that they broadcast. This is to avoid large inconsistencies in amplitude and transient spikes for their listeners. This means that you don't need to compress your track until it has no dynamic range. Average level rather than peak level determines our perception of loudness. But if everything is loud, then nothing is loud. Dynamic variation has a strong effect on our emotional response to loudness. Leave it to the broadcasters to compress your song too much. You can't stop them anyway.

Loudness Wars
Matt Mayfield

In particular, if your intended use for the track calls for a compressed format like MP3, you can filter out some frequencies that will be discarded anyway by the compression process, at the very high and low ends.

Pay particular attention to the beginnings and ends of your audio tracks. Make sure that the start of music comes immediately upon pressing Play but has a natural ramp into the wave form and doesn't sound chopped. Similarly, the end of the file should come after the full decay of sound is finished.

As always, use your ears. And then use your ears more. As Duke Ellington said, "If it sounds good, it is good." The reverse is true too.

You should be ready to deliver your finished product in any of the standard file formats via the Internet. I often will send an MP3 for evaluation by email, then once approved, upload uncompressed audio to Dropbox and send a link for download.

Some standard requested formats are:

- For video and film production, common practice is to use 48 kHz.

- Another common high resolution standard is 44.1 kHz/16 bit, which results in a file size of 10 MB per stereo minute.

- For webcast, you'll need MP3 at a bit rate that makes the file size manageable, especially if you are providing multiple versions. An MP3 bit rate of 320 kbps (kilobits per second) is my choice, if possible, as it sounds much better than the lower bit rates. The file size reduction relative to a WAV or AIFF is less than if a lower bit rate is used, but the higher quality is well worth it.

Your client may want any or all formats delivered: You should be ready to provide 48 kHz or 44.1 kHz, 24 bit or 16 bit, WAV, AIFF, MP3, or M4A. Make sure to bounce to a high resolution file, then convert to compressed version if needed, and archive them both. You'll be glad you did, if you're asked for the hi res later!

CHAPTER 4

Library Music

One segment of your market as a commercial music composer is the music library. Whether it be a specialty library that publishes only tracks in one genre, or an all-things-to-all-people library that has thousands of tracks in every style, making music for a music library to distribute can be a fun outlet for your creativity. The most important unique element to this market is that once published by one or more libraries, your tracks can be sold to end-users over and over again indefinitely. Even if the per-sale revenue is low, over time, as your published catalog expands, this can be a welcome addition to your income!

WHAT IS A MUSIC LIBRARY?

A *music library* is a company that publishes music for use with broadcast advertising, video, film, or any production purpose that requires a music underscore. Library music, also known as "production music" or "stock music," is like clipart for radio and video producers. These end-users license the music from the publisher for a fee. In the standard library agreement, the publisher issues a license for a relatively low fee as the license is non-exclusive. In a non-exclusive deal, the end users understand that the same track they just licensed may also be used in someone else's production.

This kind of product was originally called "needle-drop music," because it was distributed on LP vinyl records. The agency, video producer, or other user would drop the needle on the music track they wanted to license so as to record it to multitrack tape for mixing with other audio before "laying back" (syncing to film or videotape). After LPs went out of style, the libraries began offering collections of tracks on CD. The contemporary delivery model is to offer downloadable royalty free (or rights-protected) tracks online. The download format varies from MP3 to uncompressed WAV or AIFF files. Sound effects are often offered individually or in collections by this type of publisher as well.

The Production Music Association (PMA) is a trade organization for composer/producers and music libraries. They lay claim to over six hundred music publisher members, including major labels and independents.

Production Music Association

THE MUSIC LIBRARY BUSINESS MODEL

Music libraries receive revenue from two sources:

1. **Licensing.** Libraries charge their customer license fees for permission to sync a particular track to a piece of film, video, or other media. The amount of the fee can vary widely depending on terms and the use. A video or TV producer can download a non-exclusive track for a few dollars or pay in the thousands to use a track exclusively in a network broadcast show or ad.

2. **Performance Royalties.** Public performances of works generate revenue called "performance royalties." These are collected and distributed by performance rights organizations (PROs) such as BMI, ASCAP, and SESAC. Large "blanket" royalty fees are paid annually by radio and TV networks and stations to PROs. In the United States, the PROs collect a written record of what music was played from the broadcaster, and when and where it was played. They then calculate an amount owed to the rights holders for those performances. Next, they divide the associated revenue into two categories: one half to the writer of the music and one half to the publisher. Finally, they add up the royalties owed to each publisher or writer member, and four times a year, pay the accumulated royalties. It is reasonable and common for the music library to receive the publisher's share and the composer to receive the writer's share. A limited use of the music on a local radio station may yield a modest amount, whereas repeated use on a network show over a period of years can produce many thousands in royalties over time. Depending on the deal made with the composer, the library may offer tracks "royalty free."

Who Buys and Uses Library Music?

The purchasers of library music include anyone who syncs music tracks to productions, from ad agencies to video producers, radio and TV stations, TV networks, all the way to individuals creating home videos of weddings, vacations, or creative projects for posting to YouTube.

How Does a Music Library Acquire and Pay for Content?

There are a number of types of deals that libraries make with composer/producers. The deal may be *exclusive* in that only that library has the right to sell the tracks, or *non-exclusive* in that the composer can sell the tracks via other distributors as well. They may pay a one-time fee to own the music outright as a work-for-hire, or pay a smaller fee to license the music for resale. They may invite composers to upload music to a site designed for that purpose and pay by sharing revenue from end users who download the tracks or purchase CD collections.

Let's take a more detailed look at three common library practices:

1. Crowd sourcing with revenue sharing

2. Fee-based exclusive *work-for-hire* (the purchaser owns all rights to the work) commissions

3. Fee-based non-exclusive commissions

Crowd Sourcing

The most common business model for stock music libraries is crowd sourcing of an online distribution site. These sites get their content from producer/composers uploading their own tracks and "packages" at will or after approval by the website.

This method for acquiring content was originally a business model for photo collections. Getty Images, iStockPhoto, and 123RF are good examples, where stock photographs can be downloaded inexpensively. Photographers contribute images to these sites and share in the revenue from sales of their work. The "RF" in 123RF stands for "royalty free." This means that once downloaded for a one-time fee, the user of a royalty-free image doesn't have to pay royalties for use in particular markets or media or time frames, as opposed to *rights-managed licensing*, which is based on usage. The royalty-free license is for use in an unlimited number of ways for a single license fee. These photos often turn up in print ads and television ads.

In the case of stock music, the library maintains a website where a music producer can create an account, upload tracks, and share in the sales revenue, commonly in the range of 50 percent. Once again, the licenses they offer can be royalty free or rights-managed. Some sites exercise quality control in the form of an approval process for each track. Some sites allow contributors to upload to a site dedicated to their tracks alone and permit them to add graphics and contact information as well to help with promotion. There are many such sites. At this writing, examples include StockMusic.com, Pond5.com, Audiomicro.com.

 **Stock Music**

Commissioned Work-for-Hire Productions

Another way for a library to acquire content is by directly commissioning tracks from a composer for a negotiated one-time fee. The music library will ask for a collection of tracks of a certain genre from a composer as a work-for-hire. They then own the work and most or all of the associated rights. The library can then license the work to their clients at will, as many times as they like, without sharing the revenue. In regard to the agreement between the library and the composer, this is an exclusive contract in that the composer receives a fee and cannot resell the work, but the composer may retain some or all of the writer's share of the performance royalties.

An example of this kind of deal is the twelve-song album project *Strings*, written and produced by the author and David Mash. The *Strings* collection was commissioned by a major music library. Below is Schedule A from the agreement outlining the requirements for the album, specifying a five-version track package for each song. Note the level of detail:

SCHEDULE "A"

To the Agreement Between (Publisher) _____

and

Peter Bell, David Mash, and Bell Music

Dated the _____ day of _____, _____

The musical composition referred to herein shall be identified and of the duration as detailed below.

One (1) album of music shall be composed, in the Easy Listening/Acoustic category. The album shall consist of 12 themes and shall be delivered to the Publisher as WAV stereo audio files no later than _____,_____,_____ (date).
Each theme shall be 2:30 to 3:00 minutes in length, and have a fully orchestrated ending, with no fade-outs. Each theme and track shall either build to a positive crescendo and accent, or have a definite musical resolution. The music provided will not be MIDI or electronic sounding.

Each of the musical compositions shall incorporate 60 second, 30 second, and 15 second versions of each theme.

The five versions for each will be as follows:

       1) 2:30–3:00 full theme

       2) 2:30–3:00 full theme alternate mix

       3) :60 version

       4) :30 version

       5) :15 version

FIG. 4.1. Schedule "A" Easy Listening / Acoustic Contract

Non-Exclusive Commissions

A somewhat different type of library deal is the non-exclusive commission. This is a fee-based agreement in which the library pays a fee for the right to license the work as many times as they wish, once again without splitting or even sharing any of its revenue with the composer, for a one-time fee. The agreement between the library and the composer is non-exclusive, however, so composers have the right to sell the same music again and again through other libraries or market it in any other way they choose.

Here's an example of this kind of agreement:

Contributing Composer Agreement

Publisher: [MUSIC LIBRARY], a [STATE] limited liability company, of [ADDRESS] ("Publisher").

Contributing Composer: [Composer Name], [Composer Address] (individually and collectively "Contributing Composer").

This subject matter of this Agreement is a certain song titled: "[Song Name]" ("Song").

Grant of License: Contributing Composer grants Publisher non-exclusive, irrevocable, and transferable license, right and permission ("License") to distribute, license, sub-license, sell and otherwise authorize the public performance of Song as part of Publisher's music library ("Library"), which is made available to Publisher's customers pursuant to Publisher's then-current End User Music License Agreement ("License Agreement"). The current License Agreement is attached hereto.

Representations and Warranties: Contributing Composer warrants and represents that Contributing Composer:

a. is the sole and exclusive owner of the sound recording and composition of Song; and/or

b. is the sole composer/performer/creator of Song; and

c. the execution of this Agreement by Contributing Composer and Contributing Composer's performance hereunder, will not be in violation of any laws, statutes, state or federal regulations, court or administrative order or ruling, nor will it constitute a breach of any contract or agreement to which Contributing Composer is a party.

Non-Exclusive: Both parties acknowledge that this Agreement does not transfer any right in or to the copyright to Publisher. Contributing Composer reserves the right to grant permission to others to use the Song, upon any terms and conditions Contributing Composer desires.

Unending: Both parties agree that from the date of the execution of this Agreement, the Song will be a part of the Library of Publisher and its successor companies in perpetuity and may be sold according to Publisher's then-current License Agreement.

Transferable: If Publisher's music is bundled in a collection of other songs, or resold within a distribution network, Publisher may distribute Song through said channels. Subject to the limitations set forth herein, this Agreement is freely assignable by Publisher in whole or in part, it being the intent of the parties that any assignee of Publisher shall receive all of the rights and assume all of the obligations of Publisher set forth in this Agreement. No change or alteration to Publisher's License Agreement shall affect any rights granted hereunder, providing Publisher shall use reasonable efforts to ensure that the substantive terms thereof are not altered.

One-Time Fee: The one-time fee paid by Publisher to Contributing Composer for the License shall be: $_____ ("Fee"). Contributing Composer shall not be entitled to any additional consideration whatsoever in connection with the Song.

Arbitration: Any dispute arising under this Agreement shall be promptly submitted to and heard and determined by the American Arbitration Association pursuant to its commercial arbitration rules in effect at the time of any dispute. The determination of the arbitrator shall be binding on the parties, shall not be appealable, and judgment on the award rendered may be entered in any court having jurisdiction on the matter. The prevailing party (as determined by the arbitrator) shall be entitled to recover from the other party all costs and expenses (including but not limited to attorney fees) incurred in enforcing its rights under the arbitration process. The arbitration will be held in [COUNTY] County in the State of [STATE].

Performance Rights Organizations: Song may be registered with Contributing Composer's Performance Rights Organization, with Contributing Composer as the writer/composer, and Contributing Composer shall be entitled to retain any royalty fees to which it may be entitled related thereto.

Attorney Review: Contributing Composer acknowledges that Contributing Composer has consulted with, or after consideration has elected to waive the opportunity to consult with, an attorney with knowledge and experience related to the subject matter of this Agreement and the record and music and entertainment industry. If Contributing Composer has not consulted with an attorney, Contributing Composer represents and warrants that Contributing Composer is relying upon its own business judgment with respect to the negotiation and execution of this Agreement.

Publisher: [MUSIC LIBRARY]   By:_____

Manager:_____   Date:_____

Contributing Composer:_____   Date:_____

Printed Name of Contributing Composer:_____

FIG. 4.2. A Non-Exclusive Fee-Based Composer Agreement

CHOOSING MUSIC LIBRARY SITES

For better or for worse, when you upload your music to a music library site, you are partnering with them, so choose carefully. Before you seek commissioned work, which may take time and effort to develop, it makes sense to get started by partnering with crowd-sourced online music library sites. Not all sites are created equally, so a few things to consider when choosing are offered here.

- Ease of Use
  - Is the contributor user interface clear and easy to work with?
  - How much time will it take to upload and catalog your tracks?

- The Agreement
  - Exclusive or non-exclusive?
  - Royalty free?
  - What share does the composer receive of revenues? 50/50 or?

- Payment Terms and Policies
  - How often are payments made to composer/contributors? Monthly? Bi-annually?
  - How are payments made? Check? PayPal? Direct deposit?

- Peer Review
  - What do other contributors think of the site and the partnering experience?
  - Does the site pay on time?
  - Do they have a good sales record for their contributors?

A subscription-based resource for exploring these issues and others is MusicLibraryReport.com. This online paid service contains a list of over three hundred music libraries with contact information and reviews from composers.

Keep in mind that this site does not list all potential library site distributors for your music. If you do decide to become a subscriber, once you are familiar with the site, it's important to do further research of your own on an ongoing basis. Browse the music libraries from a Web search. Check out the deals offered, the terms, and the reviews.

Here's a :60 example of me getting in touch with my inner New Orleans on one of my library tracks, featuring me on bass and guitars and the great Amadee Castenell on tenor sax.

15. New Orleans Funk
Full

CHAPTER 5

The Library Music Track Package

INTRO TO TRACK PACKAGE PRODUCTION

Defining the Music Library Track Package

The industry-standard music library product is an instrumental composition arranged and produced as a "track package." This typically consists of five individual arrangements/mixes.

- full length (approximately 3 to 3.5 minutes)
- alt mix (alternate mix of the full-length version, with melody and solos muted)
- :60 (sixty-second arrangement)
- :30 (thirty-second arrangement)
- :15 (fifteen-second arrangement)

The long form is for film and video editors to use in creating longer productions. The shorter versions are for producers cutting TV and radio spots to the pre-timed tracks. Clients assume, and normally require, that all tracks have the exact same tempo.

Some general guidelines regarding package production:

- **Instrumentation may vary by genre.** Keep in mind that the package is designed to supply both a stand-alone soundtrack and an underscore or music bed under narration or other spoken word. The "alt mix" will be focused on narrative sections, usually dropping melody sounds that may draw the listener's attention and fight a VO.

- **Composed short endings are preferred.** If you fade the ending, make it an additional version/mix to the main submission.

- **Make all musical transitions well defined.** Editors like to cut to well-defined articulations in the music, especially at the end of the piece.

- **Create technically clean beginnings and endings.** Make sure never to chop the audio at the top and to include the full ring out of audio at the end.

- **Name the track appropriately.** Be prepared to give the track an appropriate name that evokes the style and feel of the piece.

- **Provide sorting and search information for the package.** The publisher will ask you for descriptive terms, style, genre, etc.

- **Keep note of the bpm (beats per minute) and the exact length of mixes.** This information is required by the publisher and used in their promotion of the track.

- **Make sure that all five arrangements, including any alternate mixes, have exactly the same tempo.** It's tempting with modern production capabilities to change the tempo of a composition when adapting different arrangements to particular time constraints. However, editors like to be able to create their own audio edits to fit their picture. Whether cutting picture to the tracks or adapting the tracks to fit an edited picture, if the tempo has been varied to create the various lengths, they won't have the consistency they need.

- **Avoid drawing undue attention to the music via conspicuous composition or arranging techniques.** Time signature changes and internal tempo changes all can distract from the primary task of stock music: to provide steady predictable mood enhancement.

Keep in mind that these guidelines are generalizations. I've sold tracks before that don't adhere to all the guidelines!

Here's an example of music library technical specs from the contract for an album of easy-going acoustic guitar music I composed and produced for a highly successful library. Note that in this case, the full versions at 2 to 2.5 minutes are a little shorter than the norm.

SCHEDULE "A"

To the Agreement Between _____

and

Peter Bell and Bell Music

Dated the _____ day of _____, _____

The musical compositions referred herein shall be identified and of the duration as detailed below.

One (1) album of music shall be composed, in the acoustic guitar category. The album should contain music that is relaxing, romantic, easy listening, bright and happy, and/or suited for accompanying travel and leisure productions. The album shall consist of 10 themes, and shall be delivered to the Publisher online no later than _____. Each theme will be 2:30 to 3:00 minutes in length, and will have a fully orchestrated ending, with no fade outs. Each theme and track should either build to a positive crescendo or accent, or have a definite musical resolution. The music provided will not be MIDI or electronic sounding, and it will feature different guitars and guitar styles.

Each of the musical compositions shall incorporate 60 second, 30 second, and 15 second ("stinger") versions of each theme. (It is imperative that the duration of these shorter versions be exact.) Each of the broadcast tracks will need to be composed and recorded live, not created through digital editing.

The actual end note of the 60 and 30 second versions should take place as follows:

1. for a 1 minute piece: at between 58.5 seconds and 59 seconds
2. for a 30 second piece: at between 28.5 seconds and 29 seconds.

In either case, a 1 second ring off should follow. The ring off can linger beyond the end of the 1 minute or 30 second piece, if this provides the piece with a natural ending. The ring off must not be faded out; this process will be done by the Publisher during the final mastering stage.

An alternate version or rhythm track will also be provided for the full length version. The five versions for each will therefore be as follows:

1. 2:30–3:00 full theme
2. 2:30–3:00 alternate version or rhythm track
3. :60 version
4. :30 version
5. :15 stinger

All themes will be delivered with documentation that indicates the number of beats per minute (bpm) for the composition.

FIG. 5.1. Schedule "A" Acoustic Guitar Contract

Starting Track Package Production

The first step to creating a track package to market to music libraries is to make a practical composition plan. You may be able to find out what a particular library is looking for, and if so, you're off and running. Otherwise, base your plan on your best judgment about what will be most popular and your own particular strengths as a composer/producer.

- **Genre.** Most composers have a particular style they grew up with, or that they are drawn to. Begin with a genre that you are an expert in.

- **Atmosphere.** Will the track be peaceful or aggressive? Whimsical or serious? Conventional or edgy? Knowing where you are going will help you get there. Of course, creativity sometimes takes you to an unexpected place, and your plans change!

- **Instrumentation.** Choose from the instruments or virtual instruments that you play well or are played well by collaborators whose services you are able to enlist.

- **Resources.** Think about the loops, samples, plug-ins, and virtual instruments (VIs) that you think you might use, and prepare your DAW environment appropriately. This really can help the work flow once you begin the composition. Once I pick a genre, I often instantiate a number of VIs that I think might come in handy so as to be able to audition them for various roles in the arrangement quickly and easily. Some DAWs enable the user to save custom templates for this purpose to save time when starting a new project. If yours doesn't, you can just create your own files to duplicate and use as templates.

- **Tempo.** This is an important element of your atmosphere. To begin planning, an approximate tempo range is fine. Once you're into the composition, you may want to change the tempo incrementally to fit your song to 60 seconds. Don't count on changing it much, though, as that will alter the mood.

- **Form.** Once you have a musical idea, block out a potential form that will work to length in your preferred tempo. Typical form elements include pickup, intro, verse, prechorus, chorus, bridge, drop or interlude, and outro. Or you may organize your music around typical four- or eight-bar phrases, and describe the form as is also done in poetry, for instance ABA or AABA.

- **Starting with the :60.** Correct timing is vital to the process of creating a track that may be used for broadcast advertising. A second too long or too short will render the track unusable. For this reason, when composing, you have to keep timing considerations in mind constantly. In my experience, the best way to tackle a track package is to start by composing the :60. Once you have the timing right for the :60, the longer and shorter arrangements of the song can be generated efficiently. This is my personal preference; every composer will develop their own technique.

When starting with the :60, you have, depending on your tempo, enough time to have a choice when it comes to form. Of course, you can through-compose your piece to create a 60-second-long A section. You may decide that an AB scheme works well and that it gives you a chance to make each section approximately :30, giving you a head start on the next arrangement. Other approaches that work well are ABA or ABAA. There are many ways to slice a pie. ☺

Why :60 = :59.5

The first thing you need to know about composing to length for TV and radio advertising is that all defined-length tracks should be created one half second shorter than their description calls for. The reason is that TV and radio broadcast standards require a quarter second of silence at the top and a quarter second at the tail for switching to and from other broadcast elements. For music producers, this means that the music should end in such a way that all sound including reverb decay should be finished to allow a total .5 second cushion. So, when it comes to tracks designed to be used for broadcast advertising, a :60 is really 59.5, a :30 is really 29.5, and a :15 is really 14.5.

If this standard is not followed, the music may well be abruptly cut off at the end of the spot, as the station transitions to the next broadcast segment. This result is less than professional, to say the least!

Not all libraries are detail-oriented in their requirements, but some certainly are.

Choosing Your Tempo

We'll refer to tempo in the standard way, in beats per minute (bpm), written using the convention "mm = 120" (meaning "metronome marking" or click = 120 bpm). The tempo range should be a function of aesthetic considerations. However, technical considerations may help determine the exact tempo within that range. The style, mood, meter, and pulse will help determine a possible tempo range.

Most music is written between 40 and 220 bpm. Keep in mind that bpm of 120 with an eighth-note pulse has the similar level of activity as a bpm of 60 with a sixteenth-note pulse. A hip-hop or funk track with a sixteenth-note pulse will work at mm = 60 up to 100 but may start to sound too fast at higher tempos. Samba has a sixteenth-note pulse and is commonly between 96 and 104 bpm. A sixteenth-note club dance track may fall in the 100 to 120 range. A bebop piece with an eighth-note pulse will still sound appropriate at mm = 190—or even higher, if the players can cut it.

Tempo will also be an important determinant of atmosphere or mood. It's worth noting that some classical tempo markings have a direct mood connotation, for instance "Grave" (25 to 45 bpm) means "slow and solemn."

Once you have your tempo range in mind, you can start to write your piece and see where it takes you. Pay particular attention to the ending, as that is the tricky part. One method that works well is to start to create the musical idea using a particular tempo, then place your song-position pointer (playhead) at 59.5 seconds and simply look at the Bar/Beat parameter in your transport or sequencer timeline to see how many bars and beats your tempo is giving you.

Alternatively, if you like to plan ahead, there are some practical steps that you can take to determine the number of bars and beats that you have to work with, and even to forecast the placement of your last note. To make a rough estimate of number of beats for your :60, simply determine the optimum tempo for the style you are writing in. Your bpm will by definition be the rough number of beats in your :60. Don't forget that you still have to consider the pesky half-second that we need as a cushion for broadcaster transitions. For instance, at mm = 128, our piece must be 127 beats long, including the ring out. That means that we need the sound off at beat 4 of bar 32.

As you plan, keep in mind that musical phrases are most often two, four, eight, or sixteen bars long. An uneven number of bars can work at times, however, using arranging techniques such as a pickup, intro, interlude, and outro vamp or reprise.

Trimming a Bounce

When bouncing your mixes, take care to create audio files that have a clean start, without excessive silence at the top, and a full clean ending at the tail. You may have your own routine to accomplish this task, but here's what I do to make sure my mixes are complete and ready to publish.

1. First, select a start point a few seconds before your music when setting bounce boundaries in your DAW. Then select an end point that leaves a cushion after any audible audio at the tail. This way, you won't run the risk of chopping off part of the first note or chord, or any audio material at the end, including reverb decay, as you bounce.

2. Once the bounce is done, open the bounced mix in an audio file editing window. Navigate to the beginning and tail ends of the wave form, and fine tune your selection. Be careful that you have the entire audio material highlighted.

3. Zoom in to make sure you have all the audio. Then trim your file. Now, the beginning of the file is safely at the beginning of the music without any extra wait time when we press Play, and we can hear the full beginning and end of the piece.

USING FORM TO MANIPULATE LENGTH

Never change the music's tempo when deriving various length arrangements for a track package. Video editors need a consistent tempo between versions so that they can switch versions as needed without having to adjust picture segments that have already been sync'd. Creating the different lengths without changing tempo can be challenging to the composer/producer, but in many cases, we can use musical arranging techniques to make the process easy and efficient. The most effective way to do this is to understand the form of our piece and use it to our advantage to create the elements of the track package. We may repeat form elements to make longer versions and delete or cut to make the shorter ones. Keep in mind that editing the multitrack version, with attention to individual tracks, is almost always preferable to editing a finished stereo mix. Save separately all alternative multitrack finished edited versions as you develop the package, in case you want to return to them later.

Let's see what the issues are, as we use cut-and-paste in the DAW environment to generate the rough arrangements in various lengths, then fine tune them to make sure that they time out correctly.

Beginnings, Endings, and Form

We'll assume that when you originally produced your piece, you started with an arranged beginning. When you designed the ending, you may have finished anywhere in the last measure, without a ring out to a full bar. This follows the standard client direction to end on an accented short note or chord, with an approximate one-second ring-off.

Again, it's my practice to start each package by producing the :60. In any case, whether you're expanding to create the full-length version or cutting to create the shorter versions, you'll run into issues having to do with beginnings and endings.

Intuitively, it seems that it ought to be easy to cut a :60 down to a :30 arrangement, but in most instances, it's not so simple. If you place your song position pointer perfectly half way through a :60 DAW arrangement and cut, the chances are that you won't get a fully coherent musical :30 arrangement, because if you take the first 30-second segment that you cut, you'll have a turnaround or transition or through-composed material in the last couple of bars; you won't have your composed ending. If you take the second 30-second segment, it may work in some cases, but chances are that you won't have a clean beginning. Additionally, in cases where your form doesn't have an even number of sections, you'll be cutting in the middle of a section. Furthermore, in many cases—for instance, if your :60 has a pickup at the top or a tag at the tail—cutting at :30 seconds may not be cutting on a bar line.

Let's look in more detail at some options using a twelve-bar blues tribute track I recorded in the style of Robert Johnson, the great Delta blues guitar genius.

 16. Mr. Johnson :60

We'll consider the simplest case first. The :60 form for this is AA, with no pickup or tag. The first A has a clean, coherent beginning and the second A has a defined ending designed so that sound is out at 59.5 seconds. One strategy for quickly deriving a :30 is to try to preserve the beginning and ending you've already created for the :60. This may mean taking some bars from the top and the rest from the last A.

You'll be cutting twice: once inside of the first A, then again within the second A. Then you can join the beginning and end to make one full :30 comprised of an A section with a defined beginning—one that doesn't sound abrupt or "chopped"—and also the defined ending that meets the library music standards. Any splice point that works musically is fine as long as you preserve the chord progression and the melody. The resulting length should be close to the required 29.5.

Note that when editing audio segments that are cut on bar lines, the region or clip boundaries will need trimming so that the ramp-in of audio isn't chopped and that there is no unwanted audio at the end. The screen shots are from Logic, but the principles are the same in any DAW.

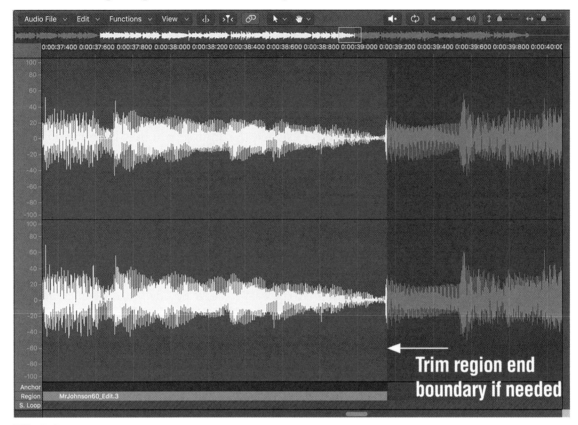

FIG. 5.2. Region Trim

As you can see, when we cut the region exactly on a bar line, it will need trimming to avoid unwanted material before we copy it to our composite :30 track.

Next, we'll cut the :60 again at bar 17 to create the second segment of our :30. Once again, we need to clean up the segment before using it in our :30. Once trimmed, always be careful when copying to maintain exact time-line position for sync, and also to use crossfading of region boundaries when needed.

Then, we can create a new track and begin to assemble the :30 by copying/dragging our two segments.

FIG. 5.3. The Initial Edits

The arrangement works well, but when we check our length including the last note and the reverb decay, it turns out to be just a little long—about :30 instead of 29.5. Just to be safe, we can make one more edit. Let's cut on the last accented chord, remembering to trim the region as before.

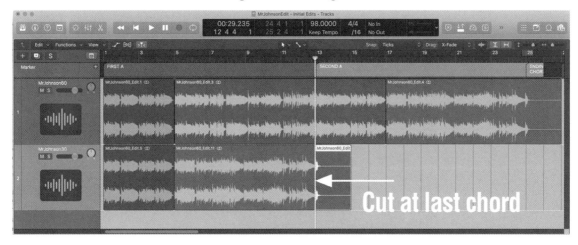

FIG. 5.4. Cut at Last Chord

After cutting the chord, we can nudge it earlier in time:

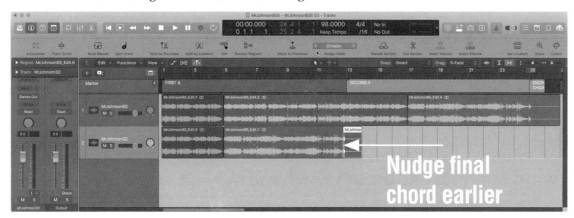

FIG. 5.5. Nudge Final Chord Placement

We can move this chord forward in time one beat to beat 4 of the final bar and still have a musical ending. Now, our length is safely at 29.5. We need to do one more thing to ensure a smooth transition: add a crossfade to smooth the transition.

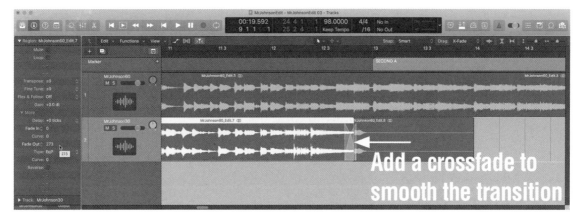

FIG. 5.6. Adjust Crossfade

When joining two audio regions, a crossfade can do wonders to make the transition sound natural.

Next, we render the edit to a new complete audio file by merging or bouncing in place:

FIG. 5.7. The Finished Edit

Finally, we can bounce the result, shown in figure 5.7. We've created a :30 arrangement from our :60 without any additional recording.

 17. Mr. Johnson :30

Using the First and Last A of AABA

Let's take a quick look at a 32-bar form with four 8-bar sections comprising AABA. Because it has an even number of segments with no pickup and no tag, the 30-second mark will fall on the bar line between the second A and the B section. If your :60 has an AABA form, simply cutting half way through will mean that you end up with either a first section, AA, which doesn't have a useable ending, or BA, which has the ending you need, but you'll be starting your :30 with the B section. Sometimes, this works musically, but if it doesn't, then the simplest solution is to join the first A and the last A.

The usual trimming and crossfading strategies will always apply, with the additional option of adjusting the fade on the final chord. Things get a little more complicated if your :60 has an uneven number of sections, or a pickup or tag. For instance, in an AAA or an ABA form, you'll need to cut in the middle of an A or a B or create new material in order to come out right.

Other Editing Techniques

If your form isn't symmetrical, you may have to resort to other techniques to make standard length arrangements.

These may include:

- Adding or dropping a pickup
- Adding transition material
- Altering the ending
- Adding a tag (in the traditional sense: a reprise of the final musical phrase)

What not to do: as mentioned, don't resort to changing the tempo of the different tracks to fit the length requirements. Video editors need all versions to have the same tempo so they can port edits and have them fit perfectly.

Track Package Production Summary

As mentioned, I've sold a number of commissioned albums for library clients. In addition, I've written and produced around forty track packages in recent years at my home studio, using Logic as my DAW. There are a variety of styles from rock to swing, blues to bossa nova. I've used a wide variety of tempos from 80 to 160 and everything in between. Most are 4/4, but a few are in other time signatures. Most, but not all, have used triggered samples for the drum tracks with some loops and live percussion thrown in. Most have virtual instruments mixed with live acoustic and/or electric guitar and sometimes live bass. Occasionally, there are live horns or other acoustic instruments.

All in all, the one thing they all have in common is that they were created using lots of trial and error, relentless effort, some mistakes and out-takes, and lots of editing and processing, all with the philosophy of doing the best job I can with the resources available at the moment and having a lot of fun doing it!

SEARCH CRITERIA

Choosing Keywords, Genre, Tempo, and Other Metadata

Most libraries offer extensive search capabilities. An important task to tackle before you publish your track package is the creation of a detailed description for the music library to use to promote your music and make it easier for people to find your music via search. This data may include the genre, tempo, mood, instrumentation, or any relevant keywords or search tags you think fit.

The best approach is to put yourself in the shoes of the video producers who visit a site to search for a track to license for syncing to a specific production. They will have an idea in mind and will be listening to a number of possible choices. However, they'll definitely want to narrow down the search to a certain tempo range, style, dynamic level, or atmosphere.

Tips on Creating Keywords and Descriptions

Here are some tips that online crowd-sourced sites typically offer their composer/ producer contributors on providing search criteria.

Tags

Tags (or "keywords") will direct searching clients to your track. The more accurate tags you attach to your track, the more searching clients will be exposed to it.

- **Specificity.** Provide as much specific information as you can. Tag the genre, the instrumentation, the atmosphere. Use any unique descriptive language you feel represents your track the best. For example, don't just identify the track by "guitar." Specify whether it's an electric guitar, an acoustic, a slide guitar, etc.

- **Emotion.** Tagging adjectives that describe the emotional atmosphere of a track is very important. Buyers will often use emotional adjectives in their search queries. This method also separates tracks that are within the same genre but evoke different feelings. For example, under almost any genre, there may be one track with tags such as "soulful, heartfelt," while another song could be tagged with "inspiring" or "uplifting."

- **Visual image.** If you feel your track evokes a certain visual image, this is useful information to the client who can use your track to help them bring that kind of image to life in their own productions. If you feel your track would be perfect for someone making a surfing video, attach the tag "surfing."

Description

Write brief but detailed descriptions for your tracks. Unlike tags, the description allows you to freely describe your track using complete sentences. This is where the artist may convince buyers that this piece is perfect for their project. Be pithy or funny or flowery, but show your conviction that the piece is great.

Here's one from my collection that doesn't mince words!

Title: "CzeckIt"

Description: Feel the passion of the dancers around the open fire. Eastern European intensity featuring acoustic guitar, balalaika, bouzouki, accordion, violin, and percussion.

Fig. 5.8. Sample Track Description

Genre

Select both a genre and sub-genre. Choosing an accurate genre and sometimes sub-genre will allow your track to be discovered more often.

All the online libraries have an "iTunes" style genre list for customers to browse through. Here is a typical music library genre list.

Aerobics	Funk	Rap
Ambient	Gospel	R&B
Animation	Hip-Hop	Reggae
Blues	Holiday	Rock
Children	Industrial	Ska
Christian	Jazz	Specialty
Classical	Latin	Spots
Corporate	Loops	Swing
Country	Metal	Television Scores
Country Rock	Music Bed	Trap
Disco	Music Cues	Urban
Dubstep	New Age	Workout
Easy Listening	News	Variety
Electronic	Old West	Video Games
Experimental	Opera	Vocal
Film Scores	Orchestral	Wedding
Folk	Pop	World

There is no doubt that good descriptions and keywords for your tracks have a big impact on sales. The following list of general concepts will help you to fill out your descriptions. It's paraphrased from a list of tips by Mark Lewis, CEO of Partners in Rhyme, a very well-run music library. If you cover most or all of these categories in your description, plus add a little flare and creativity, you will end up with a great description that compels the customer to click on the Play Preview button.

Here's what Mark Lewis suggests that we convey to the customer:

- genre: jazzy, fusion, Latin, rock, speed metal

- tempo: up-tempo, moderate, slow

- feel: funky, laid back

- instruments used, with descriptive adjectives: real guitar, swirling synths, majestic strings

- emotion: sad, lonely, happy, soulful, lost

- use: children's show, wedding video, corporate presentation, Hollywood blockbuster

- structure: is there a bridge, is there a chorus, is there a breakdown, etc.?

- reference: name some artists whose music might be similar to your track.

Customers love descriptions! It makes it easier for them to browse and gets them interested in the tracks before they even hear them. Remember that customers typically use the Search function of royalty-free music websites. If your description only says "rock song," it may not stand out, or be found, or purchased.

Here are some useful classifications, followed by examples.

Category

- Classical
- Pop
- Children's

Style or Genre

- Reggae
- R&B
- Jazz Swing

Song Types

- Ballad
- Standard AABA
- Lullaby

Interpretive Descriptors

- Soulful
- Energetic
- Laid Back

Atmospheric Descriptors

- Happy
- Sad
- Scary

Instrumentation

- Orchestra
- Big Band
- Acoustic Guitar and Vocal

Concrete Descriptors

- Gender: Male or Female Vocalist
- Tempo: Fast, Medium, or Slow
- Dynamics: Loud or Soft

It's fine if these types and classifications become conflated or mixed. The distinction between genre and style, for instance, is not always meaningful or important. No worries; all the information is useful and should be helpful in a search.

For more description and search criteria examples, check out my page at musicloops.com.

 **Music Loops**
Peter Bell

Here's an excerpt from my library track list. The full list is nine pages long!

Tracks Written and Produced by Peter Bell

1. **"Amity"**

   Genre: Folk/Country/New Age

   Keywords: Folky, country, warm, acoustic guitar, easy going, passion

   Description: Feel the vibes from this lovely homage to friendship. Acoustic guitar, acoustic bass, piano, drums.

2. **"Autumn Red"**

   Genre: Country/Country Rock

   Keywords: Dramatic, warm, emotional, inspirational, hope, nostalgia

   Description: Evocative of a drive on a beautiful fall day in the American west. Electric and acoustic guitars, drums, bass, electric piano.

3. **"Beantown Shuffle"**

   Genre: Blues

   Keywords: Shuffle, blues, lead guitar

   Description: Get down and dirty with this slammin' blues-band romp. Bass, drums, electric guitars, electric piano.

4. **"Best Friend"**

   Genre: Country/Folk/New Age

   Keywords: Warm, easy going, pretty, passionate

   Description: Lay back and enjoy this warm paean to love. Acoustic guitars, piano, bass, drums.

Fig. 5.9. Library Track List (Excerpt)

THE COMPOSER ACCOUNT

Each of the crowd-sourced online music libraries has a protocol for creating an account and uploading music for sale. Some sites ask that you submit tracks for approval. Usually, once you have a composer account, you can upload your tracks whenever ready and able.

Often, the FAQ page is where the library will describe in detail the rights and compensation deal that they offer composers. A typical site policy is paraphrased here.

How do I become an [ONLINE LIBRARY NAME] artist?

In order to be considered for artist status, you must complete the application process and provide links to your music for assessment by our company. Make it clear that you sell original production music that you have created.

Once approved, you may begin uploading your music. Each track will still need to be approved on a track-by-track basis.

Fig. 5.10. Sample FAQ

PUBLISHING A TRACK PACKAGE
Preparing Tracks for Publication

Regardless of the type of library deal you pursue, you will prepare your finished packages for publication. If you start by creating a composer account at a crowd source site, for instance, before you upload, you'll need to determine the format requirements. One of the things I do when I complete a package is to gather the tracks into folders containing various formats. If I produce a package using WAVs or AIFFs at a sample rate of 48 kHz and a bit rate of 24, I'll gather those tracks into a folder. Similarly, I then convert tracks to 44.1/16 in a second folder, and finally MP3 and M4A in their own folders. This can save a lot of time when uploading to crowd sourced sites, as you may choose different formats for different sites.

Amity MP3	ChuckIt WAV 44.1/24	MauiWaui MP3	Stadium WAV 48/24
Amity WAV 44.1/16	CzechIt MP3	MauiWaui WAV 44.1/16	TbirdTime MP3
Amity WAV 44.1/24	CzechIt WAV 44.1/16	MauiWaui WAV 48/24	TbirdTime WAV 44.1/16
AutumnRed MP3	CzechIt WAV 48/24	Montana MP3	TbirdTime WAV 44.1/24
AutumnRed WAV 44.1/16	EasyTime MP3	Montana WAV 44.1/16	TemptMe MP3
BeanTownShuffle MP3	EasyTime WAV 44.1/16	Morning Sun MP3	TemptMe WAV 44.1/16
BeantownShuffle WAV 44.1/16	England MP3	Morning Sun WAV 44.1/16	TemptMe WAV 44.1/24
BestFriend MP3	England WAV 44.1/16	MrJohnson MP3	Texas Shuffle MP3
BestFriend WAV 44.1/16	England WAV 44.1/24	MrJohnson WAV 44.1/16	Texas Shuffle WAV 44.1/16
Big Easy MP3	FunkItUp MP3	Nashville MP3	TheTrainHome MP3
Big Easy WAV 44.1/16	FunkItUp WAV 44.1/16	Nashville WAV 44.1/16	TheTrainHome WAV 44.1/16
Blue Yonder MP3	FunkItUp WAV 44.1/24	Nashville WAV 48/24	
Blue Yonder WAV 44.1/16	Golden State MP3	New Orleans MP3	Utah MP3
BluesGuitarToolkit MP3	Golden State WAV 44.1/16	New Orleans WAV 44.1/16	Utah WAV 44.1/16
BluesGuitarToolkit WAV 44.1/16	Golden State WAV 48/24	New Orleans WAV 44.1/24	Utah WAV 44.1/24
	Gullwing MP3	Rio MP3	Wellness MP3
BluesGuitarToolkit WAV 48/24	Gullwing WAV 44.1/16	Rio WAV 44.1/16	Wellness WAV 44.1/16
	Heartland MP3	SatNightShuffle MP3	Wellness WAV 44.1/24
Carlito MP3 48	Heartland WAV 44.1/16	SatNightShuffle WAV 44.1/16	WhatsUp MP3
Carlito WAV 44.1/16	Heartland WAV 48/24		WhatsUp WAV 44.1/16
Carlito WAV 44.1/24	Living Large MP3	SkyBlue MP3	Whiteout MP3
Carlito WAV 48/24	Living Large ToTIME	SkyBlue WAV 44.1/16	Whiteout WAV 44.1/16
Carljam MP3	LivingLarge WAV 44.1/16	Spirit MP3	Whiteout WAV 48/24
Carljam WAV 44.1/16	LivingLarge WAV 48/24	Spirit WAV 44.1/16	WutsUpDock MP3
ChuckIt MP3	Love Ride MP3	Spirit WAV 48/24	WutsUpDock WAV 44.1/16
ChuckIt WAV 44.1/16	Love Ride WAV 44.1/16	Stadium MP3	WutsUpDock WAV 48/24
	Love Ride WAV 48/24	Stadium WAV 44.1/16	

FIG. 5.11. Part of My Collection of Track Packages. Organized in folders by name and format.

CHAPTER 6

Direct-to-Business: Creative Concept and Pitch

Direct-to-business work differs from ad agency work in that the music house takes on added responsibility. It's important to define the relevant concerns we'll have when we sell tracks directly to a business, when there is no ad agency. In this case, the music house is writing the copy and the lyrics. We are selecting the genre of the music, and designing the campaign. We are not just following the campaign guidelines given to us by an agency; we *are* the agency. And so, to serve in this role, we need to understand the essential concepts and goals of advertising.

Every business person knows that you have to spend money to make money. Promotion is one of the costs of doing business, whether it's a multi-million-dollar car dealership or a small pizza shop. A local entrepreneur may wish to establish a brand in their local community that associates their name with quality, customer service, or other characteristic that they perceive as a particular strength. They may wish to increase sales by increasing their market share in relation to their competitors or by expanding the local market. They may, however, have a limited advertising budget that can't support the services of an advertising agency. That's exactly where we as commercial music producers may find an opportunity to sell an original jingle or track with voiceover copy of our own design directly to a client.

ADVERTISING STRATEGY FOR DIRECT-TO-BUSINESS CLIENTS

If you are going to successfully market your product directly to a business, you must demonstrate an understanding of the principles of marketing and the advertising process in general. You must also be able to apply these principles to the particular needs of the business. The key to this is to put yourself in the shoes of your potential client.

To promote a business effectively, one must:

- Set the advertising objective.

- Establish the budget.

- Create the message.

- Select the media for distributing the message.

- Hire, direct, and consult with content creators and producers.

- Buy media distribution, including broadcast air time if desired.

- Evaluate the results and amend the strategy if it needs improvement.

Let's say a business wants to increase brand awareness and increase sales/ market share while limiting their advertising budget to 10 percent of annual sales. They need a focused message that establishes their identity while differentiating their product or service from their competitors.

With a limitation on how much they want to spend, the first budget decision they'll face is whether or not to hire an advertising agency to plan and implement their campaign. An agency can provide a creative team that consists of a copywriter, an art director, and a media production coordinator (agency producer), supervised by a creative director and backed by a team of account executives and media buyers. This is a relatively expensive proposition for a small business.

If the business hires an agency, then they will not be a potential direct client for independent vendors. If you pitch a business that is working with an agency, they will refer you to that agency. However, a business might instead decide to forgo the agency option as too expensive and manage their own promotions. In this case, they hire vendors directly, such as graphic designers and broadcast music producers. They can use the products from these vendors when they buy ad space in local publications and broadcast time on local radio and TV stations.

Publications and radio and TV stations have local sales teams that are well informed about their local markets. They typically offer their own inexpensive production services. For instance, a radio station can create an affordable spot for a small business by having a staff announcer or disc jockey read copy with a library track as accompaniment. They can even add sound effects, and mix the spot using inexpensive in-house gear. To compete with this service, you will be offering something unique: original music tailored to your client's goals. You'll have to convince your potential client that even though they have lots of choices, this is their most effective use of their advertising budget.

OTHER PROMOTIONAL TOOLS AND RELATED EXPENSES

When you approach a business directly, be aware that you are competing for ad dollars that could be spent on other promotional strategies. There are many media choices by which an advertising message may be distributed. Let's take a look at some of the options, along with associated expenses, that a small business will consider when allocating promotional resources for their campaign. You'll recognize some of them from the list of choices presented in an earlier chapter regarding promoting your own commercial music business.

- **Flyers and handouts.** Expenses include graphic design, copywriting, printing, and distribution.

- **Direct mail.** Expenses include media (postcards for instance), graphic design, copywriting, printing, and postage. Additionally, a local address list may be purchased from a direct mail vendor that specializes in creating and maintaining lists targeting a particular demographic group.

- **Promotional gift items.** Imprinted pens, refrigerator magnets, calendars, etc., all also known in the music business as "merchandise" (or "merch"). Expenses include the gift item, graphic design, imprinting cost, and distribution.

- **Print advertising.** Expenses include graphic design, copywriting, and ad space.

- **Point-of-purchase display.** Expenses include graphic design and copywriting.

- **Billboards.** Expenses include graphic design, copywriting, and ad space.

- **Signage.** Expenses include graphic design, production, and installation.

- **Website.** Expenses include production elements, design, hosting, and maintenance.

- **Web advertising.** Expenses include graphic design, copywriting, and ad space.

- **Telemarketing and unsolicited email.** Expenses include scriptwriting, marketing lists, telemarketing fees, and email service fees.

- **Broadcast radio and TV advertising.** Expenses include copywriting, production (which may include voiceover talent, studio time, and/or music creation), and broadcast time.

Most businesses try some or all of these promotional tools at one time or another. Some businesses use all of them, some only a few. The decision regarding which tools to use is part of the coordinated effort known as a *campaign*, which blends decisions about the cost effectiveness of tools with creative concepts regarding the products or services of the business.

Once we have made contact with a decision maker in their organization and convinced them that broadcast advertising is their most cost-effective path, we can work together with them to define the parameters that must shape their campaign. Who is the client targeting? What are the selling points? What is the brand by which they are known by their own clients?

IDENTIFYING THE TARGET AUDIENCE

In order to create an effective campaign, the first thing you must know is whom you are targeting. Who are the potential clients of the business? What is their location, and how large is the area they live in? What media do they watch or listen to? What kind of music do they like? If you can pinpoint your audience, you can tailor your message effectively.

The Demographic

When this type of information about people is gathered and organized, it is called a "demographic profile," or simply a "demographic." For an ad agency or business that can afford it, demographic information of an area is available from market research firms for a fee. In many cases, the target audience may be obvious. For instance, if you are selling cars, you won't target people under sixteen.

In some cases, target audience information is less intuitive. This is the specialty of the writers of the Freakonomics franchise: videos, articles, books, and blogs. For example, if you are marketing a leisure activity, their data suggests that you should target people who are unemployed, on the theory that they have more time and are looking for escape from their worries!

Freakonomics "What do people do when they're unemployed"

A demographic profile of your potential customer may include:

- gender
- age
- marital status
- education
- income bracket
- location
- life stage (e.g., new parents, etc.)

Psychographics

Psychographics are a less concrete set of characteristics about your target audience. These are personal characteristics of the group, including:

- attitudes
- values
- interests/hobbies
- lifestyles
- behavior

For example, if you are a rollerblade store, you may target students and employed young professionals of all genders who have an active lifestyle, are under the age of thirty-five, and live within twenty miles.

Most established businesses are already well aware of their current clientele and their target audience. This is reflected in their current print and broadcast advertising, which should always be a vital part of your research about potential clients.

ORGANIZING THE MESSAGE

No matter what promotional tool is used, a campaign will involve messaging in the form of copywriting. It may be graphics and print, song lyrics, voiceover copy, or a dramatic script. In every case, the message is designed to promote the brand in general, or a specific product or service. The message should include:

- name
- location
- phone number or other contact, such as a URL
- list of attributes or selling points
- call to action
- slogan or tagline

Brand

Branding is a special kind of messaging. How does the business want to be identified? What do they want their image to be? What is their personality? The answer to these questions constitutes the set of associations that go with a company and is known as a "brand."

We often think of large multinational corporations, when we think of branding. One that I've done spots for in the past that comes to mind immediately is Nike. We see our sports heroes wearing the Nike "swoosh" logo every time we watch a sporting event. As a result, when we think about Nike, we associate it with particular characteristics: young, energetic, daring, and stylish. When we have done spots for them, our task has been to create music that evokes these qualities, such as this track that Chris Rival produced for us featuring the great guitarist Duke Levine.

18. Nike "Anton"

Another brand competing in that same space is Converse. We did a track that I love for a Chris Evert Converse spot, "You Marry Him," in which we recorded improvised scatting over a track by our ace composer/arranger Tom West, sung by the great jazz singer Rebecca Parris. In that spot, Converse portrayed tennis great Chris Evert as the embodiment of the Converse brand. In keeping with this, we were mindful of creating a piece of music that was active, exciting, sophisticated, and upscale.

19. Converse Evolo

Another example of branding is Chevy's strategy to associate their company with traditional American values. In the last twenty years, this has been reinforced with familiar songs, including the licensing of Bob Seger's "Like a Rock." Chevrolet has been pursuing this strategy since the 1950s, as exemplified by Dinah Shore singing "See the USA in Your Chevrolet."

Any business can build brand awareness through their promotional efforts. Music can play a major role in branding a company. A key component of evoking associations is choosing the right style or genre of music.

An example is a jingle I produced for a direct-to-business client, Olly Shoes, a children's shoe provider that features custom foot measuring and fitting. Without an ad agency creative team, I was lucky enough to get lots of valuable input from the founder and CEO, Katherine Chapman, about what she wanted to convey with the music. The branding message is written specifically into the lyric, "Olly is all about fit and fun." Their tagline said it all: "Shoes Fit for a Kid."

I worked closely with Katherine to craft a full-sing jingle with music and lyrics that conveyed their selling points and kid-friendly spirit, including that tagline. It won't set records for musical innovation, but sometimes, that's not the first priority. I had the idea to use children's voices, including a way of singing "Olly Shoes" evoking the playground with a "Na na na na na na" melodic ditty at the end, to reinforce the child-centric identity of the company. We recorded in old friend Larry Luddecke's studio. The vocals were handled by Mike Payette, with a "kids chorus" provided by Larry's own children with direction from Jon Aldrich. Jon has done hundreds of jingles, and I always learned a lot from working with him. He has the technical skill to write out his arrangements, but most of the time, he just comes up with harmonies on the spot, sings each part to the vocalists, and leads them in performance. His great personality and easy-going leadership style helps as much as his technical skill and his freakishly talented ear. Here's our track for Olly Shoes.

 20. OLLY_FS_:60

Selling Points

What specifically can a business say about itself to make it seem attractive and differentiate it from the competition? Here are some possible points of differentiation for a pizza shop.

- **Product.** "We have the most delicious calzones on the east side."
- **Price.** "Nobody sells for less."
- **Location.** "Conveniently located near the town square commuter rail station."
- **Hours of operation.** "We're the only pizza store open 24/7 in Smallville."

Call-to-Action

A call-to-action is a very important component of your advertising message. To be effective, your call-to-action should be simple, clear, timely, and urgent. For example, a pizza shop might say, "All calzones half price this Sunday only from 1:00 to 3:00 p.m. at Smallville Pizza. Don't miss it!"

Often, the listener is asked to call the business's phone number. In the classic Empire Carpet TV jingle campaign, the call to action is simple and direct. We hear the vocal chorus sing "800-588-2300, Empire," then the voiceover, "Jump up and call us, right now."

 Empire Carpet Commercial

TAGLINE

The most important part of the message that you are crafting for your client is a short, memorable catchphrase or slogan that will work with or without music to associate the listener with the product or brand. This is the phrase on which you'll base your musical hook, vocally or instrumentally. Notable familiar successful examples include McDonald's, "I'm Lovin' It" and Coke's classic print and jingle slogan, "It's the Real Thing." This type of phrase is known as the "tagline."

A high-quality tagline will do the following:

- **Include the product's benefits.** A great tag line may stress a beneficial characteristic like permanence or healthiness.
  ○ "A diamond is forever." (DeBeers)
  ○ "Eat Fresh." (Subway)

- **Stay true to the advertiser's identity.** The line must be compatible with the personality or brand of the advertiser.
  ○ "Think Small." (VW)

- **Keep it short and simple.** The Nike tagline is a classic, short, and to the point.
  ○ "Just Do It." (Nike)

Here's an example that's too long:
  ○ "The best connections in the world mean nothing if an airline forgets the human one." (Iberia Airlines)

- **Avoid complexity.** Here's an example that's too complex. It's hard to understand on first listen.
  ○ "Where we succeed is helping you make the most of your success." (Shawmut Bank)

- **Stay positive.** An upbeat friendly message is best. The jingle using this slogan is decades old and is still in use.
  ○ "Nationwide is on your side." (Nationwide Insurance)

- **Be memorable.** This following line has eight words—over our limit. However, its message is so simple, so powerful, and so compelling that it is instantly memorable. It is expressed as an admonition, but this important message couldn't be more positive.
  ○ "A mind is a terrible thing to waste." (United Negro College Fund)

PITCHING A JINGLE DIRECTLY TO A BUSINESS

Before you can help someone with their advertising goals, you must identify them as potential clients, make contact, and make the sale. Let's look at some practical steps for finding and pitching clients.

- **Finding Potential Clients.** Check local publications, TV, and drive-time radio to see and hear which local businesses are already spending for promotion, and who they are targeting. If you know any local business owners personally, that's a great place to start!

   It's worth recording and analyzing the spots you hear before you approach a local business. Once you have listened to their current spots, you will already have a good idea of what they want to convey to the market. If they are not using a jingle already and relying instead on stock music with a voiceover on top of it, they are a good candidate for your service. Researching and understanding their current advertising will give you a huge advantage when it comes time to offer them the value added of a custom-designed memorable song for their business.

- **Making Contact.** You can save a lot of time and energy by making your first contact on the phone. If your call is taken and your potential client is interested, then asking for an in-person meeting can be the next step. Ask to speak to the person in charge of advertising. In a small business, this may be a busy owner/operator, so don't hesitate to get to the point.

   Identify yourself and the reason for your call: "My name is [*your name*]. I'm a local music composer/producer, and I think I can make your broadcast advertising more effective, *and* I can do it without adding much to your current budget."

- **Pitch Your Unique Value.** Confirm that their current broadcast spots are produced by the local station using a voiceover with stock music. Make the point that this type of production is missing one highly important ingredient that the local broadcaster does not have the expertise to create: the sung vocal.

   As a music composer/producer, a jingle is what sets your service apart and adds unique value. A voiceover on top of stock music will never be as memorable as lyrics delivered in song form with a musical hook associated with the name and slogan of the business.

NEGOTIATING A PRICE

The entrepreneur may be surprised that a custom-made jingle could fit his budget. Instead of fixing a price ahead of time, ask the client what they can afford.

In general, your fees as a song composer/producer will differ from project to project as a function of your expenses for the particular job, the time it takes to complete it, and the value that you put on your skill and experience. The invoice that you send will list musicians' and vocalists' session fees, voiceover session fees, studio time, any media or other materials used, special expenses like travel or shipping, and last but not least, the creative fee. In the advertising world, this fee is charged for any creative process—in particular, coming up with the concept for a campaign. In the case of the music house entrepreneur, your creative fee is your compensation for being the composer and producer of original music for your client.

You will submit a written bid, itemizing the charges and setting the terms of payment. Usually, you will require a deposit to cover your expenses. The balance will be due on satisfactory delivery or "net 30" (in thirty days). We will cover this vital aspect of your music business in more detail in chapter 12. For now, suffice it to say that when pitching to a small business, you'll want to make sure your bid is affordable.

If the client is buying airtime already, then they probably have an advertising budget of at least a few thousand dollars a month. A one-time cost in the neighborhood of a couple thousand dollars for a custom jingle that they can use for years should be relatively affordable for them.

If you think it will help your cause, offer a free demo. If they don't like it, they don't pay a cent. This means, of course, that if it doesn't sell, you will not recoup your expenses. But remember, whether they buy it or not, this song can be added to your reel.

CHAPTER 7

Songwriting for Advertising

One key feature that a jingle producer has to offer to a business, that sets his product apart from all other broadcast ad producers, is the custom-made musical logo, also known as the "hook."

Nothing is more compelling and memorable than a pleasing melody, especially when sung by the human voice. We are universally drawn to songs as small children, and the appeal never diminishes. Our preferences regarding style and genre mature as we do, but our emotional response to melody and song endures for our whole lives.

When you offer a custom song to a direct-to-business client, you are offering a unique service that no non-musician can give: a unique, musical, vocal phrase that will be associated with their business or product alone. Your potential client may be surprised and very interested to hear that this service is readily available without going through an ad agency, and even more surprised to discover that it's actually affordable.

TIPS ON WRITING JINGLE LYRICS

If an agency is involved, the copywriter from the creative team will either provide a set of lyrics or work with you to develop lyrics from a set of selling points or branding message. If you are hired directly by the business, you'll be working with the entrepreneur collaboratively to develop lyrics. The client may never have attempted this before and will usually rely on you as the expert.

Let's look at some concepts to keep in mind when writing song lyrics.

- **Rhythm.** The lyrics must fit an easily singable rhythmic pattern. A quick and easy way to create singable lyrics is to use a familiar pop song as a template. Pick an existing song with a successful melodic rhythm and sing your lyrics using the same rhythm instead of the original song lyrics. If your lyrics work well in that context, you know that they can work well when you create your original melody for your client. Just make sure that you don't wind up accidentally plagiarizing anything in your final version!

- **The Chorus.** The verse of a song will have different lyrics each time it occurs. The chorus will have the same lyrics each time. Reserve the most important and consistent identifying information and selling points for the chorus. Often, the chorus is simply comprised of the repeated tagline.

- **Figures of Speech/Devices.** Try using memorable figures of speech and language devices to enhance your lyrics:
  - Metaphor, an implicit comparison by a literal substitution: "Life is a box of chocolates."
  - Simile, an explicit comparison: "Life is like a box of chocolates."
  - Onomatopoeia, the use of words that sound like what they mean: scrape, splutter, squirt
  - Rhyme, the repetition of similar sounds: ink, slink, fink
  - Assonance, the repetition of vowel sounds: Light my fire; Read 'em and weep.
  - Alliteration, the repetition of consonant sounds: Lemon-lime; Peter Piper picked a peck of pickled peppers.

The Tagline as Lyric

The payoff of any popular song is the musical hook, which in the case of advertising usually has the tagline as the lyric. We'll dive into musical techniques for creating a hook later in this chapter.

SONG FORM

Song form for advertising is essentially "song form compressed," compared to other kinds of songwriting. Instead of having three and a half minutes (as in the case of a pop song) or longer (as in the case of an album cut), the advertising composer has one minute, thirty seconds, or even less to work with, in an advertising song.

Form describes the architecture of a piece of music. Formal analysis has evolved over time in American popular music, with the meaning of many of the terms—notably, "verse" and "chorus," quite different now than before the pop music revolution of the '50s and '60s. Here is a review of the terms in current common practice that you are probably familiar with, and that you may use when communicating with clients and other musicians, and also in organizing your compositions.

- **Pickup.** A partial measure at the beginning of the song before the full arrangement starts.

- **Intro.** A passage at the beginning of an arrangement, usually instrumental, which serves to introduce the mood, character, and tonality of the music to follow.

- **Verse.** A segment that tells the story. Usually, this element is repeated with each occurrence having the same melody but different lyrics.

- **Prechorus.** An optional transitional segment between the verse and chorus.

- **Chorus.** A segment that delivers the point of highest energy. Each occurrence has the same melody and same lyrics. In pop music, the chorus often includes the song's most appealing, catchy, memorable musical phrase: the hook.

- **Solo/Instrumental Break.** A segment without vocals, with music from any part of the form. A single instrument may play an improvised solo.

- **Bridge/Interlude.** A segment with a musical idea that provides a contrast to or "release" from the other sections. The bridge connects two segments. It often includes lyrics.

- **Drop.** An interlude with a change in texture, usually to a lower dynamic level—for instance, a passage with only bass and drums.

- **Reprise.** A short repetition of a musical phrase or segment at the end of a song, often of the final cadence of the verse or chorus.

- **Outro.** The ending passage of a song. It may be a repeating vamp or chorus from the body of the song and helps bring the song to a close.

- **Vamp.** A repeated chord progression or musical passage, often comprising the outro at the end of a piece as the song fades.

For an example of the use of contemporary form terms, here's my analysis of the form of "Every Breath You Take" by the Police.

"Every Breath You Take"
Police

FORM	ANALYSIS	DURATION (BARS)
Pickup		a single snare strike
Intro		8
Verse 1	A	8
Verse 2	A	8
Chorus 1	B	8
Verse 3	A	8
Bridge	C	10
Interlude		16
Chorus 2	B	8
Verse 4	A	8
Reprise		6
Outro Vamp Fade		~32

FIG. 7.1. Form Analysis of "Every Breath You Take"

STANDARD JINGLE FORM ELEMENTS

Let's apply these terms to common practice in advertising. When it comes to jingles, most terms are used in the conventional contemporary way. However, it's worth noting that the term "tag," which in jazz circles is synonymous with a short reprise at the end of the song, has evolved in advertising to mean the branding slogan sung at the tail of the spot over the *final cadence* (a resolving phrase or chord pattern, a musical conclusion), encompassing the message of the spot, the high point, and the hook.

Here are the common form segments of a jingle, with functional descriptions. The length of the spot will influence how many segments are used. The order may vary.

- **Intro.** Usually a couple of seconds long. It gets right to the message and lets the listener know what's coming musically.

- **Verse.** May have information that can change from verse to verse, or version to version, or campaign to campaign.

- **Bed.** The instrumental music that serves as backing for the voiceover. As we've seen when sung vocals are not present, this may comprise the entire spot.

- **Chorus or Tag.** The musical logo, usually containing the company name and slogan; the hook.

Note that "bed" and "tag" as used in this context are not really musical terms so much as advertising jargon.

Here are some standard jingle forms that you will be asked to create:

- **Donut (:30 or :60).** Sing at the top, sing at the tail, with an open bed in between for the VO.

- **Tag Arrangement (:15, :30, or :60).** An instrumental bed that serves as underscore for a VO, with a :05 to :10 tag sing at the end.

- **Tag Special Case (:15, :30, or :60).** In advertising, it is common practice to ask for the tag anywhere in the piece.

- **Full Sing (:15, :30, or :60).** Singing throughout; may contain verse(s), bridge, and tag.

In the next section, we'll see that whatever the arrangement, the payload of a song is the tagline—a 5- to 10-second segment that features a musical hook either with lyrics, VO, or graphics containing the informational components we want to emphasize, the business name, and the tagline.

CREATING A MELODIC HOOK TO EMPHASIZE A MESSAGE

Once the lyrics and tagline are written, the songwriting begins. This part of the job is the same whether you are working with provided lyrics from an ad agency or you have developed the lyrics yourself directly with the client. Paraphrasing my good friend Jon Aldrich, the jingle hook is best explained as follows: When an advertiser puts up a billboard or creates a print advertisement, they may use eye catching photography and or a clever message throughout, but almost always, the boldest, most colorful, and largest type is reserved for the name of the business, the tagline, and often the phone number. A good jingle follows the same principle. Instead of using large or bold type, you as song creator have other tools, outlined below, with which you can emphasize the most important components of the message.

SPECIAL CASE: THE MUSICAL LOGO WITHOUT LYRICS

One way to think of the melody of a song tag is to see it as analogous to a business's graphical logo. In both cases, the message can be delivered with or without words.

The Nike swoosh doesn't even need to have the name affixed. Everyone knows what it means.

The same principle pertains to logos that are musical rather than graphical. In broadcast advertising, there are musical phrases that are just as ingrained in our ears as the Nike swoosh is in our eyes.

- **NBC.** Often a musical tag once rendered with the vocal no longer needs the lyrics to remind us of the brand or product, as in the case of "The NBC Chimes." This indelible musical phrase has been in use since the 1930s!

  The NBC melody identifies the network without needing the letters vocalized. We supply the letters in our mind's ear. The three notes outline a major triad: Sol, Mi, Do. It is simple, direct, and indelible.

- **Intel.** The Intel song never had lyrics, except in the ear of the Australian composer, Walter Werzowa, who came up with the melody by singing to himself the words "Intel Inside."

  The Intel song is often referred to as the "Intel Chimes." It is played instrumentally with a rich layering of synth sounds, mostly marimba and xylophone. Alternatively, the song is sung by a chorus "scatting" the notes using a single syllable, "bum." By some estimates, this musical logo is heard somewhere throughout the world every five minutes.

- **CVS.** The Sol Re Do CVS tag is an example of a musical logo that became engrained in our ears with its lyrics, but eventually was familiar enough instrumentally to serve as a musical logo. At my studio, we didn't write this jingle, but we did have the wonderful opportunity to go to Dublin for two weeks and work with legendary producer Brian Masterson at Windmill Lane Recording Studios along with a lot of wonderful Irish musicians to produce 193 cuts using this theme, many of them instrumental tag arrangements and buttons.

What do all these familiar advertising musical logos have in common?

- **Brevity.** They contain three to five notes.
- **Consonant intervals.** They avoid dissonance. Exceptions exist, and prove the rule.
- **Resolution on Do or Sol.** They impart a feeling of completion and stability.
- **Singability.** They are easy to reproduce with our voices.
- **Lyrical implication.** The lyrics are implied, whether or not they are sung.

MELODIC, HARMONIC, AND PRODUCTION TECHNIQUES FOR EMPHASIS

Which came first, the chicken or the egg? In advertising, the words usually come first. Hopefully, whoever is writing the copy will have a musical sensibility or is using an existing song as a template, as we described earlier, in order to ensure the lyrics are suitable for a song rhythmically. Either way, the point of the music is to support a marketing message. In particular, your job is to emphasize the *billboard information*—the name of the business and the tagline.

You have distinct tools of emphasis in the three roles you play when creating a song; as composer, arranger, and producer.

As a composer, you can choose melody notes that emphasize the business name or tagline by selecting any or all of the following:

- **High note.** A high note takes more energy to sing and creates increased intensity.

- **Note of long duration.** Long duration focuses the ear on the note, and therefore the lyric.

- **Pause.** Especially when unexpected, a pause will grab our attention.

- **Melodic leap.** In a singable, largely stepwise melody a larger leap will stand out.

- **Melodic resolution.** Resolution to Do or Sol lets us feel that the message is complete, positive, and secure.

- **Harmonic resolution.** Like melodic resolution, ending on a cadence will bring us home to a sense of finality.

As an arranger, you can emphasize the name and tagline with arranging techniques:

- **Add vocal harmonies.** Adding harmony raises the energy level.

- **Change instrumentation or texture.** Adding the fullest orchestration increases energy as well.

- **Repetition.** Repetition is ubiquitous in pop music, and even more so in jingles.

As a producer, use effects and processing in the mix to emphasize name and tag, for instance:

- **Delay.** Adding delay on a specific word can draw attention to it.

- **Special processing.** Pitch quantization (the T-Pain effect), telephone EQ, etc., can give the hook more interest.

- **Sound effect.** Adding a sound effect is another way to emphasize a point.

Memorability

A *mnemonic device* is a characteristic or feature of the message or music that aids memory. It can be an association or a unique quality. Aside from standard aids to memory like rhyme, a good jingle will provide the listener with a unique or unexpected characteristic to hopefully create an *earworm*. For instance, an unexpected rhythm or chord or melodic note or interval can make a song unique and memorable. There are many techniques for making the song memorable by including something unfamiliar or unexpected. Among them are:

- unexpected rhythm or syncopation
- non-diatonic chord or melodic note
- rhythmic displacement
- dissonance
- unexpected interval or leap larger than a sixth

MELODIC ISSUES IN JINGLE WRITING

The best way to make sure a song is comfortably singable is to try singing it yourself. If you are writing for another gender, then simply sing an octave away from where the vocalist will perform the song. In some cases, when you are writing for a particular performer or group, you may write a melody that's technically difficult, but if you want it to appeal to the average listener's instinct to sing along, then "sing it or fling it." If you can't sing it comfortably, then the average listener won't be able to sing along either.

Most songs use the same basic approaches to melody as other forms in pop music:

- **Conjunct Motion.** Conjunct motion (scalewise or chromatic) is the easiest to sing. An example is the fun song for Jell-O, which is easy for us to sing. The opening (and closing) line is a great example: Sol Si La Ti Do.

- **Disjunct Motion.** As a contrast, disjunct motion (leaps) add interest and memorability. Enhance the hook with a leap.

- **The Pentatonic Scale.** Don't hesitate to use the simple pentatonic (five-note) scale. This scale occurs in virtually every culture all over the world, proving its universal appeal.

Major Pentatonic Scale

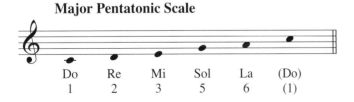

Do	Re	Mi	Sol	La	(Do)
1	2	3	5	6	(1)

Minor Pentatonic Scale

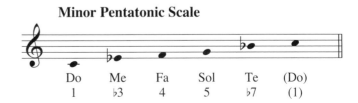

Do	Me	Fa	Sol	Te	(Do)
1	♭3	4	5	♭7	(1)

FIG. 7.2. Major and Minor Pentatonic Scales

- *Major* pentatonic scale: Do Re Mi Sol La (Do), or 1 2 3 5 6 (1).

- *Minor* pentatonic scale: Do Me Fa Sol Te (Do), or 1 ♭3 4 5 ♭7 (1).
  The McDonald's "I'm Loving It" tag is a good example of a pentatonic melody that anybody can sing. This McDonalds musical logo
  is simply the major pentatonic scale, with the last two notes inter-
  changed so as to resolve on the fifth of the key.

- **Common Intervals.** Common intervals of a third, fourth, fifth, or
  sixth are ubiquitous in jingles. However, drawing attention to your
  song with an unusual interval is an approach worth considering,
  as in the augmented fourth in the opening phrase of *The Simpsons*
  theme.

- **Memorable Rhythms or Rhythmic Phrases.** Choose a pulse that
  works for the lyrics. Let the singer breathe; add rests. If the copywriter writes so many words that there is no room to breathe, it is
  possible by overdubbing and editing to produce it, but it won't sound
  natural.

  When writing a melody to provided words, work out the rhythms
  first, usually in phrases of two or four. Give your copywriter a
  chance to rewrite the copy to a click track, or even better, a sketch of
  a rhythm in the style they are proposing.

  "What makes a Subaru a Subaru?" is a wonderful example of a
  repeating rhythmic phrase, using displacement. The syllables of
  "Su-ba-ru" first enter on beat 3 of the bar, then repeat on beat 1 of
  the next bar. Notice that once again, the entire phrase is constructed
  from the major pentatonic scale.

- **Songwriter's Notebook.** Most songwriters keep a notebook of ideas,
  which may include chord progressions, melodic phrases, and lyric
  ideas. In the case of a song producer, add taglines and three- to
  five-note melodic hooks. The notebook may be pencil and paper or
  digital, GarageBand on an iPhone, etc. (A great book on organizing
  songwriting ideas is *Songwriting in Practice*, by Mark Simos; Berklee
  Press 2018.)

  As part of your trove of ideas, it's a great idea to organize a playlist
  of songs that lend themselves to emulation for songwriting. You
  and your client may use these to great effect in the development
  process. As mentioned earlier, you can even ask a copywriter to
  use a particular song as a template for writing lyrics. This is a great
  way to increase the chances that the lyrics will be grouped in singable phrases, that you won't be asked to fit an unrealistic number of
  words into the song, and that the lyrics will have the right number of
  syllables to fit a workable rhythm.

As a jingle writer, you are not just following your own muse; you are trying to
appeal to the broadest possible audience. Musical appeal is of course subjective,
and in the "ear of the beholder." No matter what techniques you use to organize
your writing, there is one overriding principle that you should always return to:
use your ear!

CHAPTER 8

Winning an Agency Jingle Project

There is a sharp contrast between working direct-to-business and working as a vendor to an agency. In the latter case, you are writing a jingle with content and direction provided by the ad agency team. To set the scene, we'll start with the story of how Bell Music got started.

CASE STUDY: STARTING UP MUSITECH/BELL MUSIC

Musitech (now Bell Music), before we moved to Newbury Street in Boston, began as a home studio in Cambridge, MA with a 16-track, tape-based studio, before the era of digital audio workstations. Sampling and sequencing were handled by partner and tech guru, David Mash, using (among other gear) his Roland MSQ-700. My other partner, Peter Johnson, owned a couple of Shure microphones, a small mixing board, and a tape machine that he was given as part of a prior record deal. He and I had both had some modest success in the pop music world, had previously been signed to major label recording contracts, and had national touring experience. I was newly married, starting a family, and like David, teaching full time at Berklee College of Music, but I was hoping to become an entrepreneur and dive headfirst into commercial music.

First Steps

Getting started isn't easy, and my own experience is a case in point. I can laugh about it now, but it takes faith and dedication to weather the storm of rejection, low pay, and scant appreciation that are features, not bugs, of the life of a beginning music entrepreneur.

Musitech began by trying to market our music services to what was then a thriving production community making slideshows for corporate events. These days, corporate video is a huge market, which has, for the most part, moved on from slideshows, but in those days, there were companies exclusively devoted to audio/visual presentations using slides. These shows featured a computer-controlled progression of slides shown on a large matrix of screens, accompanied by a synchronized, original music track, and mixed with an announcer's voiceover and sound effects. The shows were presented in auditoriums and theaters, sometimes to the public, sometimes to company personnel or potential investors. These A/V (audio/visual) companies, as they were known, had trade gatherings and conventions where slideshow producers would gather, hand out awards, and network with peers and vendors.

A typical slide show soundtrack job was eight to ten minutes of original, through-composed music, created to a detailed spec sheet. This would consist of at least two weeks' work for a modest fee, perhaps $500.

My recollection of these early years is as a series of frustrating experiences. We took our new brochure and reel, which consisted of a cassette tape of sample tracks that we made just for that purpose, around to as many industry gatherings as we could and talked to as many producers as we could meet. The producers we approached were sometimes receptive, sometimes dismissive. We did a few jobs successfully and added them to our fledgling reel, but in more cases, the slide-show world seemed uninterested in trying us out. Sometimes, we got responses that were downright rude.

I began to think that if we couldn't make a success of the lower paying slide-show jobs, we'd never get going with the better, more lucrative jobs, like TV and radio jingles.

Getting Positioned for Success

Even though we were struggling to get started in the high-work/low-pay world of slideshows, we decided to send our brochure and reel around to the local ad agencies, although without much confidence. We didn't have a single jingle on the reel because we had never done one—not even a virtual jingle, created solely for the reel. We weren't sure who to send the packages to, so we simply called the agencies and asked to speak to someone who was responsible for reviewing music demos. In every case, we got the information we needed—not with a lot of enthusiasm, but politely. Agencies need music vendors. They usually work with established providers whose work they know and trust, but occasionally, they are open to trying out someone new if they hear fresh energy and creative talent in their demo.

By sending out our package to ad agencies, even though we weren't really succeeding brilliantly with slide show companies, we learned what I believe is the single most important lesson one can learn in business. One can never control external factors in a way that will guarantee success, but one can prepare for potential success and do everything possible to be in a position to succeed— to be ready if external factors do fall into place.

We had worked for years to develop our skills as musicians. We had a recording studio ready to produce the product we wanted to sell. We planned our business and created promotional materials and sent them out even when it seemed unlikely that we would get an opportunity. We did everything we could to put ourselves in a position where success could happen.

The Presentation

One day, out of the blue, we got a call from Hill Holliday, one of Boston's largest and most successful agencies. We were invited to come over and present our reel to the creative department.

Trying to contain our excitement, we showed up for our appointment in the fancy Hill Holliday offices, high up in Boston's John Hancock Tower. We had no idea what to expect. We were led to a smallish room, not big enough to be described as a conference room, and introduced to a copywriter named Doug Houston, who it turned out had liked our brochure and was behind the invitation. We were joined by only one other person—an art director, I believe, although he didn't introduce himself. Doug put our tape into a cassette player they had set up, and during the first cut the art director stood up and said, "Who mixed it, the bass player?" and walked out. It turned out that the playback system had the bass control all the way up and the treble turned down! Once we readjusted the EQ, Doug politely listened to the tape, and a couple of other "creatives" wandered in and out of the room as it played. Afterward, Doug thanked us for coming in. We left thinking that we would never hear from them again.

The Competitive Demo

When an agency is preparing a campaign that involves music, they will typically pay for several studios to compose and produce demos, all using the same specifications. Your demo is in competition with the others, and only one can win!

To our surprise, Doug Houston decided to try us out by including us in one of these competitions. The agency producer on his team called and said they had an idea for a song for a local bank, BayBank, and they'd like us to take a shot at it. We would be paid $1,500 flat fee for the 30-second demo (three times what we were used to getting for an 8-minute slide show), and we were in competition with two other experienced studios: one in Nashville and one in New York. They wanted it as soon as possible—the advertising agency norm. Deadlines are always tight and the pressure is always high.

Doug got on the phone and read me the lyrics he wanted for the song. He said the style should be rhythm and blues. Other than that, we were free to use our own creativity. Later, they couriered over the brief, but we were already at work.

That week, I made the worst mistake a jingle writer can make: I changed the lyrics. In fact, I changed part of the tagline. When I think about it now, I can hardly believe how naïve I was. An agency copywriter gets paid a large salary to create song lyrics. The lyrics are pegged to the concept of the campaign that is pitched to the client. The approval process is substantial. The creative director of the agency must approve the concept, the tagline, the song lyrics, and all other aspects of the plan. Then, everything is presented in detail to the client for their approval. Finally, the plan is implemented. At that point, for a jingle composer to unilaterally change the lyrics without approval is the ultimate example of "the tail wagging the dog."

The campaign was based on the idea of differentiating BayBank from the competition by highlighting its extensive ATM network (which in those days was innovative). Doug's lyrics were:

> *I've got my BayBanks Card, I'm a real go getter.*
> *My BayBanks Card, things just keep getting better.*

Peter Johnson and I recorded and mixed a version with our friend Alex Taylor (James Taylor's older brother) singing our altered lyrics. Alex was one of the best singers I've ever worked with. I absolutely loved what he did with the song.

Responding to Rejection

The response was swift. Doug was surprisingly nice about saying that he wanted the lyrics as he had written them, without alterations. He also said that the voice was wrong for the spot; they wanted something more "middle of the road." I thought we had blown our chance but asked him if we could have another shot at it. He said we could, although we'd have to work within the original budget.

Luckily, Doug didn't "bottom brick" us by asking us to change the song completely. When a client asks you to change a track in a way that means you have to start over from scratch, it's like changing the bottom brick in a building. You have to knock the building down and start over.

We were in the process of learning that in advertising, *atmosphere*—the sum of associations that a particular piece of music evokes—is as (or more) important than whether the music is hip, or great, or has a good groove, or rocks, or is thrilling.

I collaborated with our friend Ardys Flavelle to recreate the song. I played the guitar, and she tried out melodic ideas. As she shaped the melody, I provided the chords, and we worked back and forth until we had a progression and a melody that we liked.

We thought our track was pretty tame already, but we thought maybe Ardys's voice would change the feeling to a more generic friendly tone, and sure enough, she sang the song with lovely clarity and enthusiasm. And this time, we used the lyrics we were given. No changes.

Winning the Competition

To our great surprise, this time we won! They loved Ardys's voice, and the job was ours. They gave us a budget of $10,000 to produce a 30-second TV song with our song. We were thrilled, and this set the scene for us to learn another important lesson.

We thought that with such a large budget (for us), we should add more instrumentation and bring in an experienced jingle vocalist with a track record. We made a new arrangement with horns, brought in a proven R&B vocalist that had done songs for Hill Holliday before, and recorded and mixed in a bigger studio.

The Hill Holliday creative team were underwhelmed. The team at the agency had been listening to Ardys's demo over and over and had fallen in love with it. We were paid the full amount for the new version, and they eventually made a spot using it, but to debut the campaign, they aired a spot with Ardys's appealing, innocent-sounding voice—the demo virtually unchanged, although Peter Johnson had the great idea of adding Red Sox crowd noise to the mix!

Here's the BayBank piece with Ardys—the early version—with Mike Turk on harmonica.

 21. BayBank Ardys :30

Lessons Learned

Here are some lessons one can take from our first experience with an agency—from having our first BayBank demo fail, and then come back to life and win.

- **Listen to your client.** Your job is to fulfill the vision of the client. Your client is a professional with training and experience. If you have an idea, feel free to bring it up, but never assume that you know your client's business better than they do. Above all, unless invited to do otherwise, and when musically possible, use the lyrics you are given without changing so much as a single word.

- **Atmosphere is everything.** If the atmosphere isn't working the way the creative team envisions it, then nothing will work. Your direct client is the agency. They may want to be cutting edge, or they may want to aim for the middle of the road. Think of authenticity as a continuum, not a binary issue. Remember that music is subjective. Sometimes, one man's authenticity is another man's bland or generic. Be respectful, and be careful how you communicate about this. There's a chance you may offend your client if you are too frank about this issue!

- **Trial and error.** Be ready to change the song, the arrangement, the vocalist, or anything and everything—even the proverbial bottom brick. Be ready to submit multiple versions until the goal is reached. If you give up too easily, you haven't given yourself a chance to succeed. Trial and error is a great production philosophy.

- **Don't take it personally.** Rejection is a continuous fact of life in the advertising business. To succeed, you'll need to get used to it and have a thick skin. There are many reasons why your work may not be a fit for a client's needs. It doesn't mean you aren't worthy!

- **If it's not broken, don't fix it.** When a client is happy, you still may want to improve the product. But if you change it too much, you may lose something in the process that's very important: the attachment of the client to your first version. The reason pop music artists want their music to be played on Top 40 radio is that repetition breeds acceptance and affection. After lots of repetition, agency folks may get attached to the first version they hear.

GETTING TO KNOW THE AGENCY TEAM

When you get a production assignment, your first priority should be to identify and collaborate with the people who will make the decisions about your work. When your client is a TV station, a television production company, or a local business, you may be working with one key individual as a collaborator and decision maker.

When you work with an ad agency, you will almost certainly be working with a "creative team." The agency creative team will provide the brief and further direction, and often will attend the recording sessions, especially the vocal and voiceover sessions. For practical purposes, the agency personnel that you, as a music vendor, interact with will be limited to the following team members:

- **Copywriter.** Often the originator of the concept of a campaign. Responsible for writing taglines, voiceover copy, and dialog. The copywriter often originates the campaign idea, sometimes in collaboration with others in the team. They write the tagline upon which the campaign is based, and all associated copy, from TV to radio to billboards to direct mail and beyond.

- **Art Director.** Responsible for print graphics and television visual content. The art director is responsible for all things visual, including the fonts, the images used, and the look and feel of the TV footage.

- **Agency Producer.** Responsible for scheduling and negotiating with vendors, including music producers, often as part of a team with a copywriter and art director assigned to a particular client and/or campaign. The agency producer handles the financial issues, scheduling, and logistics, including travel and accommodations for the team, when necessary. The producer will be your contact for negotiating the budget and terms and coordinating session scheduling, so the team can be present if desired.

- **Creative Director.** Team leader and decision maker on creative content for agency clients/campaigns. The creative director oversees all ideas and has power of final approval. The campaign idea has usually gone through a rigorous approval process by the time a music house is approached.

You'll find approval of your work to be a two- or sometimes three-step process. First, the creative team must approve the demo. This may even happen at the session. Next, they take a mix back to the agency for the creative director to approve. If you pass this level, it's likely that you've succeeded, though the agency client (who is after all paying the bills) approval is the final step. Most of the time though, the agency client will rely on the expertise of the agency.

The final client is not typically a part of the production process, as they normally leave the details of production to the agency. There are exceptions to this rule, however. I've had to do things over before because, for example, "the CEO's spouse didn't like the singer's voice."

The organization structure of a typical ad agency includes the following:

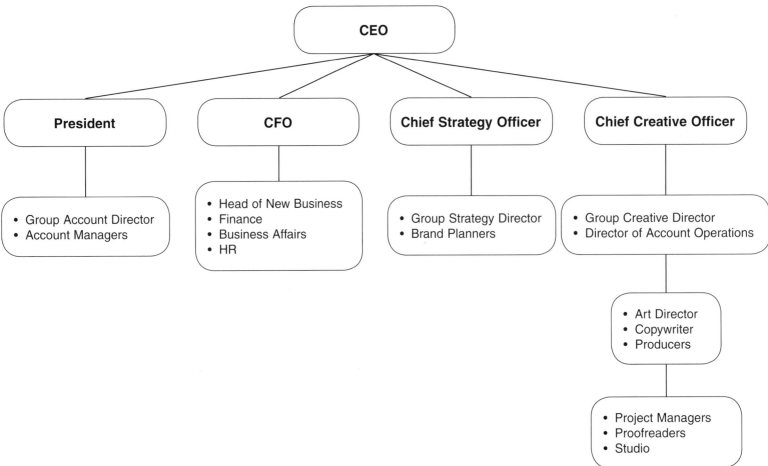

FIG. 8.1. Ad Agency Organization Chart

The agency's account representatives act as middlemen between the agency and their client, and provide support to creative decisions with practical business considerations. Like others on the business side who conduct media buying, market research, focus groups, and strategic planning, they have an important role of course, but are almost never at sessions.

THE CAMPAIGN

An "ad campaign" is a coordinated series of advertisements focusing on a common theme. A campaign may have a limited time frame or be open ended. The focus may be a particular product or service, or more generally, a brand. Campaigns are designed to reach a particular target audience and to increase awareness or market share for a business or product. A campaign is defined by the creative content, or message, and also the media delivery method used to convey that message.

For instance, let's look at a successful insurance company series, the Nationwide "World's Greatest Spokesperson" TV campaign. This campaign consists of a series of tongue-in-cheek TV ads featuring an announcer who is interviewing consumers about their specific needs and communicating the results to the company. Each image is from a separate TV spot from the campaign.

Nationwide Campaign "World's Greatest Spokesperson in the World" McKinney Advertising, Durham, N.C.

Other notable ads featuring a spokesperson or "spokes-character" include campaigns for the rival insurance companies GEICO, Aflac, and Progressive.

- **Geico:** 1999 to Present: Gecko; 2004: Caveman

- **Aflac:** 2000 to Present: Duck

- **Progressive:** 2008 to Present: Flo

Whether a spokes-character is involved or not, if you are fortunate, your song will become part of a campaign and your agency client will come back to you again and again to produce different versions. The genre of the arrangement, the lyrics in the verses, and the song form all will change, but your song will tie the campaign together.

Our BayBank song was a perfect example of this. As we mentioned, Hill Holliday was the New England ad agency that commissioned my studio to create it. Though based in Boston, they are a large agency with offices in New York, Los Angeles, and other large markets. When the copywriter who designed the campaign left to form his own agency, Houston Advertising, the BayBank account went with him, and so did our song. Over a period of years, we did many versions of the BayBank song featuring Ardys and others—some well-known, as you'll see (see tracks 21 to 25). One of the key ingredients to our success in writing and producing this song, and to spinning out these versions, was that we welcomed collaboration with the agency team with open arms.

TIPS ON AGENCY WORK

Working with Provided Lyrics

Copywriters will often use an existing pop song as a template for creating lyrics. They sing their words over the lyrics of an existing song, matching the songwriter's rhythms. If they don't, as mentioned before, you can suggest this as a good way to make sure the lyrics are rhythmically singable—the key to any good song. Of course, the exact melody can't be replicated! When the lyrics don't work rhythmically, it's up to you to point out the problem and help them fix it. Another common issue is having too many lyrics. Usually, the copywriter will work with you, but as we have illustrated, don't expect them to accept substantive lyric suggestions. This is their turf, and they have a message to get across. However, when it comes to music, you are the expert. They have as much invested in making the song singable, and therefore memorable, as you do.

Collaboration

If you have a budget, don't try to do everything yourself. We all have limitations to our talents. As we mentioned in chapter 2, when we were going over roles and responsibilities, you may be in a position where you need to try and do many things by yourself when starting out. Once you start getting paid work, though, you'll want to use the budget to involve others. You can't sing convincingly like a soprano if you are a baritone, even with Auto-Tune.

Here are some things to think about when collaborating with other musicians, composers, or arrangers.

Hiring a Composer or Arranger

As a music house, you don't have to write every piece of music that comes out of your studio. When working with an agency, you will have a budget that includes covering your talent expenses, including musicians, vocalists, and an arranger. You'll also be paid a creative fee for composing original music. You are free to use some of this fee to bring in others to collaborate in your role as composer, or even to delegate it entirely.

If a particular style or genre is required, find a specialist who knows the genre inside and out. This usually means someone who works in that genre more than any other—someone who lives and breathes the style, or grew up with it.

Don't be shy when thinking of asking an accomplished artist to collaborate on a song. In twenty years, I've only once had an artist tell me that they didn't want to work on an advertisement because it was an advertisement, and even he later changed his mind. Bonnie Raitt doesn't do advertisements, but she does public service announcements when she believes in the cause. She did a wonderful spot for us as part of a Red Cross blood drive we participated in (see track 42).

In every case that I've invited an accomplished or well-known artist into the studio to work on a commercial music project, I've been amazed at how much care and energy they put into the project. In my experience, great musicians put their heart and soul into everything that they do, even when it's for an advertisement.

Choosing the Players

Similarly, the players you choose must know the genre well, or you'll hear the lack of mastery in the final product. When in doubt, your musical collaborators may be able to recommend the right players. Composers, arrangers, instrumental musicians, and vocalists know the best practitioners in the area in their musical specialty/genre and will usually know them personally and may already have their contact information.

When Doug Houston came to us for a Dixieland version of the BayBank song, we hired Bob Winter, an accomplished arranger/pianist who we knew was an expert in the style. He immediately wrote and performed a great chart. He knew the players he wanted, and we took his recommendations. The result was a hit with the agency, the bank, and the public. Once again, Ardys Flavelle handled the vocals beautifully. At around this time, I had the mind-blowing experience of overhearing people spontaneously singing our jingle on the street, on the subway, and in a pub.

Versions of the BayBank song that we produced using different arrangers, vocalists, and musicians, included artists Livingston Taylor, Rebecca Parris, and the New Kids on the Block. Listen to the following examples to get an idea of the disparate genres involved in a campaign that lasted for years.

22. BayBank Livingston Taylor :30
23. Rebecca Parris :60
24. BayBank Ardys Dixieland :60
25. BayBank New Kids on the Block :60

CHAPTER 9

TV Theme Music

Every television show has a theme. It is the music that plays under the opening titles and under the credit role at the end and may or may not be referenced in the underscore during the show. It can be instrumental or vocal. It may be a pop song used under license, such as "Woke Up This Morning" by Alabama 3, for *The Sopranos*. Or it may be written to order by a commercial composer, like Berklee alumnus Ramin Djawadi's theme to *Game of Thrones*.

Historically, a TV theme has occasionally even become a radio hit after the fact. For instance, the *Welcome Back, Kotter* theme song by John Sebastian went all the way to No. 1. Henry Mancini's theme to *Peter Gunn* won an Emmy and two Grammys. Jan Hammer's theme to *Miami Vice* also won two Grammys and is regarded as the most successful TV theme of all time, both the single and the album hit No. 1.

"List of Television Theme Music"
Wikipedia

A fun resource for browsing and searching for downloadable TV themes is TelevisionTunes.com. The site lists almost 19,000 of them, and even has an interactive game where you can listen to themes and try to identify them. Sheet music for TV themes is available through publishers such as Hal Leonard.

CLASSIC TV THEMES

Broadcast television began to be relevant in the U.S. in 1948 with Texaco Star Theatre starring the great comedian Milton Berle, known in that era as "Mr. Television." That year, Arturo Toscanini first appeared conducting the NBC Symphony Orchestra.

The Lone Ranger

"The Lone Ranger" "The William
Tell Overture" Gioachino Rossini

In 1949, Rossini's *The William Tell Overture* was first used on television as the theme to *The Lone Ranger*. It was already familiar from the radio show of the same name, as well as a well-known piece of music from the classical repertoire.

This selection set the stage for the thousands of TV themes that came after it. It perfectly suited the spirit of the show and its hero, who often came riding in at the last minute to save the day, after which he rode off into the sunset as one or other of the characters would wonder, "Who was that masked man?" This character, this phrase, and this music became indelibly linked in American pop culture of the time.

The rhythmic figure—two sixteenths on the upbeat resolving to an eighth note on the downbeat—evokes a horse galloping. You'll hear this emulated in the classic TV theme music to *Bonanza*, as we'll show below.

Dragnet

Dragnet Theme,
Walter Schumann

Soon after, in 1951, the *Dragnet* theme composed by Walter Schumann, followed. Once again, the theme is orchestral, but this time composed specifically for the radio, and later the TV show. The show was a crime drama starring the down-to-earth, no-nonsense L.A. police detective Joe Friday.

"Dragnet" gave us the opening four notes that every kid for decades sang when mimicking a dramatic situation for comic effect: "Uh oh, here comes the principal, Dunm dah dunm dunm...."

The blaring low horns of the opening playing the minor phrase set the tone as ominous. Then the pause on the diminished fifth without resolve creates a feeling of expectation and dread for the crime drama to follow.

This theme still has cultural resonance as is evidenced by the fact that it is quoted in the tongue-in-cheek musical tag in use for the Tums "Is Your Food Fighting You?" campaign, although this version resolves to the fifth of the key instead of the augmented fourth, for more of a sense of resolution. Decades later, the theme is instantly recognizable.

Peter Gunn

Peter Gunn Theme,
Henry Mancini

The *Peter Gunn* theme became the model for cop show television and movie music for decades. Its rock/jazz fusion arrangement, driving beat, and exciting dissonance based on an F7 chord (sometimes with altered tensions) are classic. The bass line and melody are bluesy but with an odd twist—an example of Henry Mancini's unique cross-cultural sensibility.

Bonanza

Bonanza Theme, Ray Evans
and Jay Livingston

The *Bonanza* theme is a lot of fun to play on the guitar, since you can play the opening of the melody using the second, third, and fourth open strings, with no left-hand fingering until the La Ti Do at the end. Note the rhythm emulates the Rossini rhythmic figure used for *The Lone Ranger*, so evocative of galloping horses, central to the setting of the show.

The Twilight Zone

The Twilight Zone Theme,
Marius Constant

Then in 1960 came *The Twilight Zone*, a place still referenced by comedians when evoking weirdness incarnate.

This brilliant melody conveys the eeriness of the series of science fiction and macabre stories hosted, and mostly written, by Rod Serling. The dissonance is created by alternating major and minor seconds, in this case exacerbated by the use of a flatted fifth on the tonic chord, E major ♭5.

Sanford and Son

Sanford and Son Theme,
Quincy Jones

The *Sanford and Son* show was about a poor but optimistic junk dealer and his son in South Central L.A. The main character, Fred Sanford, played by the genius comedian Redd Foxx, continually hatches harebrained schemes to get rich quick, much to the consternation of his earnest and responsible son. Jones's theme conveys the cheery, goodhearted, but irascible father character beautifully. It's funky like the junk shop, but upbeat and irrepressible like the show's protagonist. The bluesy harmonica, Latin percussion, and the ratchety clavinet sound evoke the creaky nature of the shop's inventory and of its proprietor.

60 Minutes

60 Minutes
Opening Theme

This is a special case as the show has never used theme music, only the ticking of the on-screen stop-watch. At the top of the show and after every break, the ticking serves as an intro to the next segment, with the stop-watch time updated. A great example of the power of a simple, clear idea!

Welcome Back, Kotter

Welcome Back, Kotter Theme,
John Sebastian

A year after John Sebastian wrote the easygoing theme song for *Welcome Back, Kotter*, the song went to No. 1 on the pop charts. The show starred comedian Gabe Kaplan who returns to his Brooklyn high school to teach a remedial class of ne'er-do-wells, with hilarious results. The show launched John Travolta's career as he starred as one of the wisecracking students. Note the use of the slightly "rough" sounding chorus for background vocals, portraying the rough-edged but lovable members of the class.

Miami Vice

Miami Vice Theme,
Jan Hammer

This phenomenally successful theme had the dramatic high energy and danger that went with the hit show about two undercover vice cops in the drug under-world of Miami with its fast cars, fast boats, and fast money. The music, costumes, art direction, and the editing style of the show were all groundbreaking and hip for the time—including star Don Johnson's habit of going unshaven and wearing Italian sport coat, T-shirt, and white linen pants. NBC executive Brandon Tartikoff was rumored to have referred to the show as "MTV cops." Aside from being a world-class keyboardist, composer Jan Hammer was one of the first to use sampling (listen to the guitars) and synthesized drums (listen to the toms) in his scores.

The Fresh Prince of Bel-Air

The Fresh Prince of Bel-Air
Theme, Will Smith

The Fresh Prince of Bel-Air is an interesting case. Will Smith, already a successful rapper when he signed on to be the star of the show, wrote and performed the theme song. The premise and basic plot of the show is fully explained in the rap! An instrumental version was also produced and used under credits and shots of outtakes and bloopers. The music couldn't be more perfect for the show.

The Wire

The Wire Theme, "Way Down in
the Hole" Tom Waits, etc.

This great series famously used as a theme Tom Waits' gritty "Way Down in the Hole," featuring a different recording each season, starting with the Blind Boys of Alabama version, then in turn, versions by the composer, the Neville Brothers, DoMaJe, and Steve Earl.

Game of Thrones

Game of Thrones Theme,
Ramin Djawadi

Because contemporary cable series production is so varied, there is more oppor-tunity for someone who is "not in the club" to be chosen to create a theme, though the barriers to entry are still high. After graduating from Berklee, *Game of Thrones* composer Ramin Djawadi got his start working with Hans Zimmer and others on movie scores. He had graduated to scoring movies on his own when the producers contacted him to write their theme. He initially told them he was too busy, but relented, and now this theme is a classic. The atmosphere is dramatic, powerful, and romantic all at once. The theme includes leitmotifs for the major characters and dynasties portrayed in the show over the course of an unusually long intro, and as scoring during the episodes.

Is it luck, hard work, talent, or persistence that determine opportunity? It's all of the above. We never know if and when a door of opportunity will open, but we can do everything possible to be ready to walk through if and when it does.

Westworld

Westworld Theme,
Ramin Djawadi

The opening to *Westworld* is a spectacular example of visual effects married to music, with a robotic skeletal hand playing Ramin Djawadi's theme.

MNEMONIC ARRANGING TECHNIQUES

Some of the most memorable TV themes have used unusual instrumentation as a *mnemonic* device—something assisting or intended to assist the memory, so the listener can't fail to associate the sound of the theme with the program.

The 77 Sunset Strip *Finger Snaps*

77 Sunset Strip Theme,
Mack David and Jerry Livingston

The show *77 Sunset Strip* was about two L.A. private eyes solving capers with flair and humor. The show played on the cool style of its Hollywood setting. This theme from the late '50s used finger snaps to convey the show's jazzy atmosphere and "coolness" as personified by its popular hair-combing hipster character, "Kookie." The character was further immortalized in the novelty pop radio hit "Kookie, Kookie, Lend Me Your Comb."

The Andy Griffith Show *Whistle*

The Andy Griffith Show Theme,
"The Fishin' Hole" Earle Hagen

The relaxed, fun whistled melody to this classic theme, "The Fishin' Hole," was performed by the composer, Earle Hagen, himself. The song puts us in an atmosphere of natural innocence that is just right for the hit show about lovable characters in small town rural America of the '60s.

The Law and Order *"Clang"*

Law and Order Clang

The long running hit show *Law and Order* is not just famous for its theme, but it's also associated with its characteristic sound effect reminiscent of a gavel clanging down, or a prison door slamming. The effect was created by theme composer Mike Post by combining a number of clang effects and flooding them with reverb. It is used as a transitional cue (sting) to signal important plot and scene changes. The show, created by Dick Wolf, has been so successful that actor Richard Belzer has referred to the effect as "the Dick Wolf Cash Register Sound."

Multiple Performance Mash-Up

Another arranging technique sometimes used to promote a show using the theme is the mash-up of various groups of musicians or ordinary fans performing the theme. A fairly typical example is the CBS :30 promo spot for *Hawaii Five-0*.

 Hawaii Five-0 Theme
Mash-Up

All the great themes have different styles, genres, instrumentation. Some have become clichés, some have gimmicks, some stand alone as great music.

What do all the successful themes have in common? It may sound simple, but the only common attribute of every great TV theme is that the music is perfectly suited to the atmosphere of the show.

SUCCESS BREEDS SUCCESS

When agencies, music supervisors, media producers, filmmakers, or decision makers of any sort choose a composer, they often do what we all do when we choose any service provider or vendor. They look for a successful outcome that they can emulate, or a referral from a peer. This means that for the provider, success breeds more success. You'll notice this tendency if you pay attention to the actors in national spots. You'll see the same faces in commercials for various products, chosen because if they were successful in one ad, maybe they can help bring success to another. This means that if a composer gets a couple of successful jobs, they may soon become "flavor of the month." Once that happens in advertising or TV work, the phone will start to ring. If you keep performing well, you can build a reputation.

There is, however, a barrier to entry into the exclusive club comprised of successful studios. If the purchaser is risk averse, they will want to work with someone with a proven track record. This of course makes it more difficult for a new contender to get started. A counter-influence to this tendency is the aspiration on the part of the purchasers to do something fresh and new, leading them to want to give an unproven composer a chance.

Another aspect of the process that helps someone starting out is the competitive demo process. This allows for a less risky transaction for the purchaser, as all they have to lose is the time and effort involved in including a new vendor in the competition, and a demo fee, because their risk is covered by choosing proven writers for the other participants in the competition.

Because of this tendency to emulate success, many themes will be assigned to a few trusted studios unless a new player gets the attention of decision-makers somehow. This can lead to much frustration when you're trying to get in the door. It's important to keep a positive attitude and be as patient as you are persistent. You never know when an opportunity will arise as you build relationships with your work. One thing may lead to another, as you'll see in the case of my being asked to create a new theme for *This Old House*.

CASE STUDY: *THIS OLD HOUSE* THEME

FIG. 9.1. *This Old House* Logo

This Old House is a popular TV series about renovating older houses. It was founded in 1979 by producer/director Russ Morash and is still going strong, having won sixteen Emmy Awards to date. Originally created for local station WGBH in Boston, and then aired by PBS (The Public Broadcasting System), the show was owned by Time Inc. for a number of years, but is now the sole property of This Old House Ventures LLC. It is aired on multiple networks and stations, including cable network Home and Garden TV. During the PBS years, the show's theme music was a 1935 Fats Waller recording of "Louisiana Fairy Tale," written by Haven Gillespie.

"Louisiana Fairy Tale" 1935, Haven
Gillespie (performed by Fats Waller)

When Time Inc. acquired the show, they began the process of commissioning a new theme. We had done scoring and theme music for some of show creator, Russ Morash's, other shows on PBS including *The New Yankee Workshop* and *Victory Garden*. Russ liked our work and recommended to Time Inc. in New York that they include us in the demo competition.

It quickly became clear to me when Time Inc. called that the budget for this project was considerably higher than I was used to. The reason for this was twofold. First, Time Inc. is a national company and they planned to use the show on network, cable, and local television all over the country and abroad. The second reason is that they wanted a *talent buyout*—a deal that provides a higher payment up front and no future residual payments.

Usually in this situation, I would think "collaboration first." I was used to involving other musicians from the beginning of the composition process. I was sure that for the final version they would want a production with a jazz combo featuring clarinet, but I was alone in the studio when the call came in, and I was anxious to get started, so I sat down alone and wrote the song myself using my acoustic guitar.

The direction was simple and clear: create something in the same vein as the Fats Waller song. I immediately listened to the original theme, and a couple more like it by my friend, the great clarinetist and composer Billy Novick. Once I got the feel in my mind, I just let it flow. I didn't want to dwell too much on the tracks I was using as reference. I wanted to be sure to emulate but not replicate.

Those songs really got me in the right mood, and I had the new song pretty well organized that afternoon. Over a day or two, I finished the song and produced a demo by recording two guitar parts in Logic (rhythm and melody). I knew I was competing against New York studios that would submit fully produced jazz ensemble demos, but I liked the feel of the acoustic guitar piece, so I sent it in, and as it turned out, they liked it too. When all the submissions were evaluated, I was awarded the job!

For the final, we did two versions: a clarinet, piano, guitar, bass, and drums version, and a version exactly as I had written it for acoustic guitar but with added stand-up bass and drums. Both versions, and many more that I produced for them over time, aired for more than fifteen years, and are still heard on reruns.

Interpreting a Style for a Theme

It's one thing to analyze a style in the context of music alone. It's another to understand what makes us recognize and associate to elements of a particular song in the context of marrying the music to a television series. For instance, when directed to emulate Fats Waller, I could have concentrated on the fact that Waller was a virtuoso pianist, or that he was a spectacular showman and a wonderful vocalist.

However, I made the determination that those weren't the elements that the producer was drawn to in this case. Rather, it was the carefree feel of his rendition of "Louisiana Fairy Tale" and its classic nature, combined with the old-timey sound of the clarinet. *This Old House* is about renovation of older houses. There is a love of vintage architecture and design throughout the show, and an appreciation for the craftsmanship or workmanship of a time past. The viewers of the show are old enough to be homeowners, or renters. The show moves at a leisurely pace with a friendly, easy-going atmosphere.

So, my reasoning went that I was going to be concerned with early jazz, possibly bluesy, but pretty and light. Above all, it was important to use all acoustic instruments: clarinet, acoustic or "jazz box" hollow-body guitar, upright bass, drums, and piano. We also wanted to keep the atmosphere playful and cheerful.

In all cases, the principle is to understand the show, its culture, and its audience.

The Guitar and Clarinet Arrangements

For the clarinet/ensemble arrangement, I hired Billy Novick as arranger and leader. The classic jazz styles of the first half of the twentieth century—swing, Dixieland, and ragtime—are his specialty. When I gave him the song to arrange, I gave him the guitar demo recording, and my handwritten transcription of the song in the key of G, copied over because of lots of erasures. ☺

This is how the guitar version sounded once the final was recorded:

26. *This Old House* Arrangement
in G (Guitar)

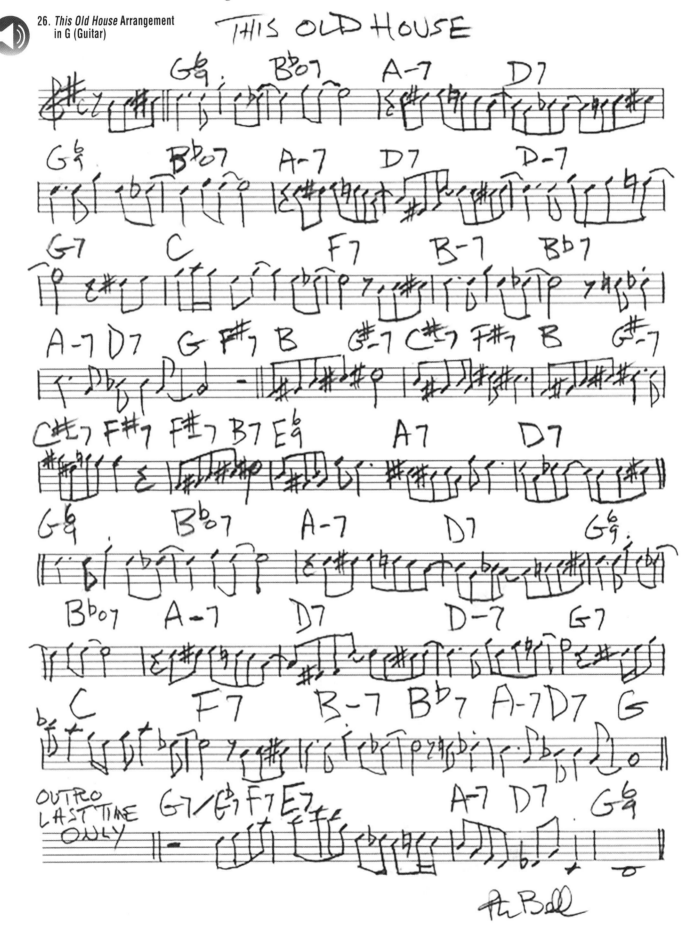

FIG. 9.2. *This Old House* Theme Arrangement in G, for Guitar

The first thing Billy did was transpose the song to E♭, a key more common to the classic jazz styles. This made it more comfortable to play on clarinet and trumpet. When we talked through the arrangement, I made a point of telling Billy that he should feel free to make minor changes in the melody, as this style was his specialty, and in the end, he did make a couple.

Here is Billy Novick's arrangement.

 27. *This Old House* **Arrangement**
in E♭ **(Clarinet)**

Billy's experience in the style was vital and gave him the expertise to choose musicians who were at home in the genre, and that he was used to working with. The performance strayed slightly from the written music as he and the other players freely use embellishments and stylistic interpretation. This is a priceless value added by experienced musicians who know the genre.

The Studio

In deciding how to do the recording, my first priority was authenticity. Even though I have many years of experience creating drum tracks that sound human and "real," for this project, I wanted a live drummer, recorded the old-fashioned way. In addition, I wanted the full session to be recorded live, with minimal overdubbing. Because of this, I wouldn't be using my home studio, where my recording booth isn't big enough for a drum set. Chris Rival and his studio was the perfect solution because he had the space for this type of recording, and he is an "old school" recordist who's a purist when it comes to acoustic sound sources and live sessions. He's expert in both analog and digital production, but to this day, in a world completely taken over by the use of DAWs, he still maintains a high-end two-inch analog tape machine and console in his current studio where he's produced many great artists.

The Negotiation

There is a natural division inherent in every music production project: the amount allotted for production, and the fee for creative service. A producer must make a realistic evaluation of what it will cost him to deliver the product, adding up estimated fees for arranging, musicians, and vocalists, studio time including recording and mixing, and any other expenses. Then comes the tough part: assessing what their time, experience, and talent are worth. Instead of starting with an artificial sense of how you'd like your creativity to be valued, let the market be your guide. In the final analysis, your service is only worth what someone is willing to pay for it. Your client will usually have a figure in mind because of a budget that has already been set, considering many factors, including past experience with similar projects and an assessment of common industry practice.

When it came time to negotiate the budget for *This Old House*, I dealt with a Time Inc. producer from New York who was very forthcoming about the company's position. In situations like this, I like to start the negotiation by asking what the client feels is fair, rather than giving a specific number as my bid. A reasonable question is, "Do you have a budget in mind?" This way I avoid bidding too low. A bid that's too high can always be amended, but if you bid too low, and the bid is accepted, you have sunk your own ship, so to speak. In this case, my strategy worked to my favor. Because Time Inc. wanted to be the publisher of the music and avoid any future talent payments (and I suppose, because they were used to paying "New York" rates), my fee and production budget was to be considerably more than I expected. As mentioned, the talent agreement was a *talent buyout*—a one-time fee that is higher than a normal session fee but is a final payout for the work. Likewise, Billy Novick was compensated commensurately for his arrangement, and for choosing and leading the musicians in the session, with the understanding that there would be no future residual payments or royalties. This necessitated work-for-hire agreements to be signed by all.

The Issue of a Theme Music Credit

Another topic I brought up was the topic of a credit. At the end of television shows, there is always a rolling display of credits for contributors of all kinds, including of course music. I was told that existing shows that were to have my music dubbed in would not be edited to include my name in the credits, but that future episodes would. Because of the generous financial terms, I agreed to this, even though I knew that credits are important for promotional purposes. True to their word, eventually a credit was added to new episodes of the show that used the theme.

In fact, after some time had passed, an item was put into the FAQ list of the *This Old House* website:

> **What is the *This Old House* theme music?**
>
> *This Old House* now has its own original theme music, composed by Peter Bell.

In addition, a nice feature was put in *This Old House Magazine* plugging the theme.

FIG. 9.3. *This Old House Magazine* Article about the New Theme

From the first phone call inquiry to the final studio sessions, there will always be a great number of decisions, judgment calls, and creative challenges. The first and most important is to realize creatively the client's vision of the musical theme. Composition, arrangement, production, technical and aesthetic requirements, budget, and promotional credit are all parts of a puzzle that a television theme provider must solve.

FIG. 9.4. Composer Credits

CHAPTER 10

Scoring to Picture

In advertising, the musical score has essentially the same function as it does for a feature film. It is a part of the soundtrack, along with dialog, sound effects, and sound design. As a commercial music producer, you may be asked to score industrial videos, point-of-purchase videos, TV spots, short films, and TV shows.

THE FUNCTIONS OF THE SCORE

Advertisements, like Hollywood films, are sometimes made with universal appeal in mind, but are more often targeted to a narrower audience/demographic. Since music house composers/producers are always writing music that is custom-designed to fit a client's vision, the process of communicating that vision accurately is vital.

Agency creatives often follow and associate their campaigns with pop culture and movies. In fact, it's common for a copywriter to reference a film score when describing the music wanted for a spot. Usually, this involves a discussion of *genre*—a loose set of criteria used to categorize a work of film or music or any art form. Establishing genre is not an exact science, by any means, but it can help start and frame the discussion with the client about scoring. Sometimes, film genres overlap, as in the case of an animated film for all ages like Disney's *Beauty and the Beast* (Children's Music, Musical) or a film like *Brokeback Mountain* (Western, Drama). In these cases, we can use sub-genres to try to clarify the overlapping criteria.

A partial list of broad film genres with their intended target audience and atmosphere might include:

FILM	GENRE	PRIMARY TARGET	ATMOSPHERIC CRITERIA
The Pink Panther	comedy	teens, adults	humor, light-heartedness
Schindler's List	drama	adults	heroism, emotional conflict
The Godfather	crime drama	males, adults	moral conflict, violence
Halloween	horror	adults	violence, fear
Toy Story	animation	all ages	animated music
La La Land	romance	teens, adults	love, song and dance
The Revenant	action/adventure	males, adults	high energy, danger, heroism
Blade Runner	science fiction	adults	futuristic, drama
The Post	historical	adults	true stories

FIG. 10.1. Film Genres, Audiences, Atmosphere

- **A good score should tell the audience how to feel.** The most important function of the score is to set the mood. You give the listeners a specific atmosphere or feeling that, in most cases, they are not even consciously aware of. The music in Andrew Bird's scores for advertisements, for example, convey youth, creativity, and upbeat, positive energy.

Andrew Bird Commercials

- **The score may function in the background without distracting from the story.** Scores are often referred to as *background music.* A great score will stand on its own as music, but in context, will never distract from the narrative it supports. An ad score may be very effective, even if after watching the ad the viewer might say, as I have heard before, "Did that ad have music? I didn't notice it." At the same time, they are likely influenced by its score!

- **The score may take a major role in telling the story.** The score may tell us the setting: the location of the narrative or the time period, as it does in the wonderful score to the film *Paris, Texas* by Ry Cooder. The movie takes place in the contemporary American southwest. Cooder's slide blues guitar evokes the dry Texas desert perfectly.

Paris, Texas, Ry Cooder

- **Another great example is Marvin Hamlisch's score to *The Sting.*** The use of Scott Joplin rags puts us squarely into the nineteenth century.

The Sting, Marvin Hamlisch

SCORING PRODUCTION TIPS

There are a number of strategies that a commercial music producer can use to bring a score alive and set it apart.

- **Use live percussion elements when possible.** It's easy and time efficient to record live claps, tambourine, or other percussion.

- **Avoid rhythmic perfection.** Human performance breathes. Nothing kills a groove like the drum-machine effect. When using MIDI controlled percussion samples, don't "hard quantize" the regions. Quantize using a percentage. If they are already quantized, then "humanize" them so that the attacks are not perfectly synced with the beat grid. Contemporary DAWs have the option to randomly skew position, duration, and velocity of MIDI events within a range to achieve a more human feel.

"Apple iPad Is Delicious"
Spot

The "iPad Is Delicious" spot has a simple and appealing composition based on rhythmic displacement. The score is based on "Never Stop" by Chilly Gonzales, from their album *Ivory Tower*." The percussion is not "hard quantized." The result is an organic sounding track. Part of the appeal is that the rhythm breathes.

SPOTTING

Spotting is the process of viewing a moving picture and deciding where the music cues or points of emphasis should go, and what they should try to accomplish. Specifically, short *cues* (musical scoring segments), or the start point or change point of longer cues, may be timed to coincide with a cut, camera zoom, shift in action, or dramatic buildup—in short, any change in scene, narrative, or dramatic content.

When creating a score for a video or broadcast commercial, in most cases, there is a back-and-forth process between the creation of the score and the editing of the visuals. The process varies considerably, but no matter how it unfolds, it has to start somewhere. There are no rules for which comes first, the chicken or the egg, in scoring. Here are some common scenarios:

1. It's common for a composer to be given a storyboard and asked to create the score to fit a series of anticipated cues before the ad is shot or editing begins.

2. Alternatively, the film or video editor may do a first cut and then give it to the composer to spot and score.

3. It's also common for the editor to work to an existing recording of published music, an album instrumental, or even a pop song, and then ask that the score be created afterwards to similar specs. Editors love rhythmic articulations to cut to, whether the score is complete or not.

Scenario 1: Create Music Before the Ad Is Shot

Let's discuss the case where the music comes before the shoot. In "Dance," a big-budget spot for Marriott International, it seems clear that the music by Mark Sayer Wade was used to sync the shoot itself and then again as a rhythmic template during editing. I'm guessing that he amended that score after the first edit, as well.

 Marriott *Dance* TVC, "Behind the Scenes"

This is a wonderful eight-minute documentary on the making of this brilliant ad, with a finished spot at the end.

Notice the subtle cultural cues in music as the dances and costumes change. The spot cycles through Argentine tango, Brazilian capoeira, ballet, Japanese dance, flamenco, and breakdancing. The basic dance pulse is the same for all. For instance, there is no literal tango music for tango dancers and no literal sixteenth-note swing hip-hop breakbeat for the break dancer. A koto-like sound enters for the Japanese dancer, acoustic guitar enters for Brazil and later for flamenco, a processed drum kit for the break dancer, and piano flourishes for the ballet dancer. No, it wouldn't work better to change the style entirely because the pulse of the dancing is continuous. The score, and the rhythm in particular, might be disjointed and confusing if the entire genre changed for each dance style. It's better to preserve the continuity of the spot.

Scenario 2: Create Music from Existing Video Edit

Next, let's discuss a case where the composer is working to an existing spot after the visuals are already edited. The first step in the process is to spot the picture.

This process may be as general as to identify the atmosphere of a scene so as to create music that will mirror its emotional arc. It may be as specific as the composer taking precise timing notes to document how long each cue needs to last, where it begins, and where it ends, while making note of particular moments during a scene with which the music may need to coincide in a specific way. The composer will identify the cuts that need transitional music, and spots that need emphasizing with a musical change, articulation, transient, or "hit point" (discussed later in this chapter).

A score may consist of music that is:

1. **Through-composed.** There is music throughout, changing to fit the action and the story.

2. **A cue-oriented composition.** The music changes to highlight events or points of emphasis. The music adheres to specific cue lengths. There may be gaps between music segments.

3. **Assorted stings or buttons.** A *sting/button* is a short bit of music or sound design created to transition from one scene or segment to another. These short sound effects or musical phrases are used to emphasize a scene change or other point of emphasis.

4. **All three in combination.** Sometimes, a score can be through-composed but have cues and stings built into its fabric.

LEITMOTIF

A *leitmotif* is a recurring theme associated with a particular identity, a person, place, action, or idea. When a certain character appears in a narrative, an associated leitmotif in the score can reinforce our perception of identity. When done well, this association becomes so strong that the theme alone can tell us if the character is nearby or about to appear, even without a visual clue. In movies, wonderful examples are plentiful. We all know the shark theme from *Jaws*, and the alien contact theme from *Close Encounters*.

- *Peter and the Wolf.* In classical music, a wonderful example is Prokofiev's *Peter and the Wolf*, in which the composer has created a theme for the hero, Peter, and each of the characters and animals in the story. The effect is heightened by orchestration—flute for the bird and oboe for the duck, for instance.

Disney-animated explanation of leitmotif in *Peter and the Wolf*

- *Close Encounters of the Third Kind.* In the *Close Encounters* theme, we hear "Re Mi Do (I) Do Sol" when humans are attempting to communicate for the first time with visitors from outer space. The idea is that music is a language so universal that even extraterrestrials understand it in the same way that we do. Note that the melody concludes with a perfect fifth, the most memorable interval in music.

Close Encounters
Theme

- ***Jaws.*** When we hear the shark leitmotif from *Jaws*, we immediately know that we should be afraid, and what we should be afraid of. The musical phrase and the great white shark become one in our consciousness. The *ostinato* (musical phrase which is persistently repeated in the same musical voice) figure comes in, a half step at first, then whole step half step repeating. The growl of the low-string octaves, and the dissonance and power are terrifying. Just when you thought it was safe to go back in the water....

Jaws Theme

Leitmotifs are found in every type of music, including advertising. As we have seen in our analysis of musical logos like the Intel theme and others, the advertising version of leitmotif may constitute a special case in that the theme may recur over a series of spots or campaigns instead of recurring in a single production. The function of the musical theme, to identify a product or brand, of course follows the same principle as leitmotif in any other form.

Here's an example in a spot we did for Freihofer's Bread featuring Matt Marvuglio on flute. The flute leitmotif underscores the narrator and unifies the score, which is juxtaposed with a series of other musical concepts for each of a variety of different characters.

28. Freihofer's :60 TV

SOUND DESIGN

For as long as humans have created organized plays and narrative performances, they have used sound to support the storyline and the emotional atmosphere being portrayed. Recorded sounds were used in theater productions in England as early as the 1890s. In 1913, the prescient composer Luigi Russolo wrote in his open letter, "The Art of Noises," that future musicians would be able to "substitute for the limited variety of timbres that the orchestra possesses today the infinite variety of timbres in noises, reproduced with appropriate mechanisms." It was another fifty years until the Moog synthesizer was released, and sixty years before personal computers were available. With the advent in digital sampling in the 1980s, sound effects have been at the touch of a key, and as digital audio workstations (DAWs) have evolved, the use of sound design using sophisticated processing is now available to all of us.

Foley

Before synthesis and sampling became widespread, filmmakers relied on studios that specialized in sound effects, called "Foley studios." Historically, these studios produced "live" acoustically recorded sounds for film soundtracks. The genre is named after Jack Foley, who began the art in 1927 at Universal Studios. The Foley artist would record, manipulate, and archive recorded acoustic sound sources that may have been produced by "acting out" plot actions, or by simulating the needed sounds in other creative ways. If they didn't have an ambient recording of a live sound event, they would stage it, or simulate it, like using a flexible metal sheet to simulate the crashing of thunder. Sometimes, a producer will prefer the Foley artist's version of a sound effect more than the real sound recorded during the action of the shoot.

"Foley Artist Explains Sound Effects" Scott Paulson

Creating sounds "from scratch" is certainly more work than finding and downloading a sound effect from a music library site. But it's a lot more fun, too. Another wonderful description of sound design is that of Ben Burtt designing the lightsaber sound effect in *Star Wars*, using the Doppler effect to evoke motion. Ben Burtt has done brilliant sound design for many movies. His explanation of his techniques is notable for their down-to-earth common sense as well as their creativity.

Ben Burtt, *Star Wars* Lightsaber Sound

HIT POINTS

Specific visual events that call for a sound effect or musical emphasis are commonly called *hit points*. The decisions you make regarding what you should and shouldn't hit are an important component of spotting. Like other techniques, this one can be overdone. Sometimes, only a few that are well chosen suffice. Hit points can be transitions, dramatic moments, or events, that require support from the soundtrack.

Our multitalented engineer/producer Chris Rival supplied the concept and slide guitar performance that made this Timberland spot a success. The music is heavy and pounding as the boots slog through the mud onscreen. Finally, the guitar slides up lightly and resolves, as a girl goes up on her toes for the hit point of the kiss (off screen).

29. Timberland :30 "Toe to Toe"

Once you identify a hit point, your next decision will be whether to use a literal sound effect (for instance, an explosion), a component of the music (like a drum fill or glissando), an articulation of the musical composition (for instance, a chord change), or an arranging technique (for instance, changing texture from a solo instrument to a full orchestration).

Perhaps the most famous film scoring technique in American film is Bernard Herrmann's use of strident violin transients to mirror the violent stabbing motion in the murder scenes of Hitchcock's classic horror film *Psycho*. Note that the violins are also designed to sound like the shrieking of a mad person.

***Psycho* Strings**

Note the effective use of contrasting dynamics as well. The score leading up to the climactic event is ever so quiet, and then suddenly jumps to maximum amplitude to heighten the horror.

Perfect Sync

When we first started doing scores for spots, I made it a practice to match my hit points in the music and effects with a specific frame. While this is fine to get you in the ballpark, human perception is such that a literally perfect sync may not be what you want. The science of psychoacoustics is complex, but suffice it to say, the best way to match an event in the score with a visual event is trial and error. Because DAWs give you the capability to play picture and music in sync quickly and easily, it's a simple process to nudge events in the soundtrack until your perception tells you that they match the visual event.

Cliché

A *cliché* is an expression, idea, or element in art that has been used to the point of becoming a stereotype. Often originally striking and creative, a cliché may become generally regarded as trite through overuse. Clichés get no respect, but they often work. In conservative genres like blues, the informed, judicious, and nuanced use of clichés is one measure of mastery. Creativity is always wonderful, but you should remember why clichés are used so often. They can be effective.

For instance, it is common to use a minor key to convey sadness, darkness, or sometimes tenderness or warmth. A parallel major key, in contrast, may convey happiness, light, or energy. This contrast is evident in the Strauss piece (*Also Sprach Zarathustra*) used as the theme to Kubrick's *2001*. The feeling changes along with the minor moving to major third of the tonic chord, from ominous to triumphant, as the extraterrestrial monolith is revealed in the opening scene set in prehistoric times.

2001 Monolith Scene

TECHNICAL ISSUES IN SCORING

SMPTE time code is a form of metadata originally developed for use in editing and synchronizing film, video, and audio tape machines. It is named for its developers, the Society of Motion Picture and Television Engineers. In the four fields of the code, every frame of a moving picture is numbered and accounted for. The standard readout will show Hours: Minutes: Seconds: Frames. The Frames field will support the number of frames per second (FPS), the frame rate, being used for that project. Since different film and video standards have differing frame rates, the final field in the display will correspond to one of several frame rates that are industry standard. The most common are:

- 24 frame/sec
- 25 frame/sec
- 29.97 (30 ÷ 1.001)
- 30 frame/sec (non-drop)
- 30 d (drop frame)

If you open an MOV or MP4 movie file in QuickTime, the Movie Inspector will show the frame rate listed (as FPS).

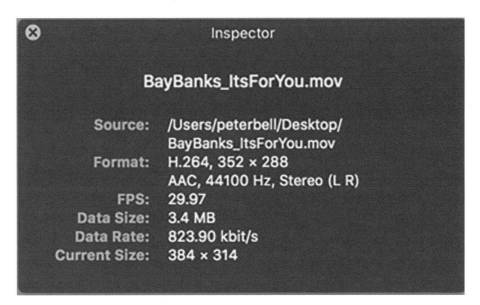

FIG. 10.2. QuickTime's Movie Inspector Showing Frame Rate

In the pre-DAW era, SMPTE was recorded onto an audio track and *burned in* (shown as text on the screen) to the video picture. The audio was routed to whatever analog tape machines needed to be synced, and you could see the burn in displayed in the picture as you spotted and scored the picture.

In scoring today, there is rarely if ever a need for the audio track of SMPTE time code. DAWs allow for importing movies and provide SMPTE display. They also provide for syncing picture starting at a particular SMPTE number with fields showing hour/minute/second/frame, and if desired, sub-frame.

FIG. 10.3. The Synchronization Preference Window in Logic.

Note that the default bar position syncs beat 1 of bar 1 to SMPTE 1 hour, exactly. The convention of starting SMPTE at 1 hour allows for movement back and forth in both time directions without having to deal with negative values.

Audio Format and File Size

Keep in mind that when you present an MP3, you are presenting a compressed file with a size reduction at 320 kbps of more than 6 to 1 relative to the high resolution original file. Compressed files can usually be transferred by email. High resolution, non-compressed files, because they are significantly larger, are typically exchanged by uploading and downloading to a server or using a delivery service intended for that purpose (such as Hightail or WeTransfer). I use a Dropbox account that allows me a certain amount of storage for a yearly fee. I can create a folder with a password that my client and I can both use to pass files back and forth. There are a number of other options available online, including Bandcamp, which gives you the capability to sync or share for free.

Even for standard CD quality (16 bit 44.1K), your audio file will take up 10 MB per stereo minute. Your client will have the audio professionally mixed to (laid back to) the picture along with voiceover, narration, ambient audio in a mix-to-pix session at a studio designed for that purpose before publishing or broadcast. This part of the process is included in the post-production phase.

You will be well served to initially present your music synced to a video file, but once it is approved, go ahead and deliver a high-resolution audio file, usually 24-bit 48K WAV.

CHAPTER 11

Subsequent Work with a Successful Score, Jingle, or Theme

PRODUCTION TECHNIQUES FOR SUBSEQUENT MUSIC HOUSE WORK

If you have written music that's working well for the client, you are bound to get the call to do new versions. Subsequent work is the result of doing a good job for a particular client, and getting the call again and again when new music is needed, whether you are rearranging your song, creating new music to order, or in some cases, doing arrangements of someone else's music that an agency has the rights to use.

My studio has been fortunate to have done a lot of subsequent jingle work, including many tracks we did for CVS, New England Telephone, TJ Maxx, BayBank, and lots of others. This work involved doing many different songs, arrangements, beds, and donuts for our clients, sometimes multiple additional versions, sometimes not.

In order to keep the advertising fresh and on point, there are a number of variables that can be updated. The advertiser may:

- **Change the voiceover.** In this case, the work doesn't include a new arrangement or even a new music track, since we were using the song without changing the lyrics. This falls into the category of post-production studio work.

  There will be no creative fee charged, just an hourly rate for the studio time involved in recording, editing, and mixing the voiceover onto the different versions.

- **Change the lyrics.** If new lyrics are required, a vocal session is part of the work. Even if nothing changes in the track except the lyrics, you might charge an arranging fee. Producing the vocals is a creative, musical process that requires your expertise as a composer/producer.

  The new lyrics are typically provided by the copywriter and should fit well with the original melody. Sometimes, the same arrangement is used, and the new lyrics are sung and mixed to the identical track. Sometimes, a new arrangement is created. If any of the words don't work musically, it's up to the composer to push back, letting the copywriter know that their new lyrics don't match the music. Arriving at a final workable lyric usually becomes a collaboration between the composer and the copywriter.

- **Change the arrangement.** The new arrangement may have new material but with elements of the original song. A typical example would be to do a Christmas version of the song, often with sleigh bells. (I have a percussion instrument solely for that.)

- **Change the music entirely.** In general, depending on the agency campaign strategy, different subsequent versions of successful songs may be required for a variety of reasons:
    - Keeping it fresh. Luckily for music houses, advertising must be constantly refreshed to attract and keep the attention of consumers.
    - Event advertising. A different sale or promotion every week is a dream for any music house.
    - New product advertising. This may be similar to event advertising as an advertiser may create new spots to feature their current inventory of products. For instance, McDonalds introduces new food choices on a regular basis.
    - Branding vs. events and products. Event (sales) and product advertising will have different campaigns than brand recognition advertising. Some of the creative content will overlap. Once again, this means more work for music houses.

Whatever the reason for subsequent work, it is a vital part of your ongoing revenue and reputation. The more the better!

SUBSEQUENT WORK FOR A TV SERIES

In the case of a series theme, your work for that client may be just beginning. In most cases, you will have the opportunity and the responsibility to create multiple versions in different arrangements and genres for new episodes of a show. You may get the assignment to create an audio toolkit for the show's producer to use in editing new episodes. This kind of work can really be the gift that keeps on giving for months or even years.

The New Brief

As we've detailed in different contexts, commercial music requires that you be a jack of all trades in that you must deliver music that fits a client's vision, whether you're familiar with that type of music or not. This is often the case when creating new versions or arrangements of a track you've already sold successfully. The client will amend the original brief, often with a different style or genre in mind to fit their current needs. Obviously, if the client says, "We're shooting a new episode in Jamaica, so I'd like a reggae arrangement of the theme," you'll need to understand the nuts and bolts of the reggae genre.

As always, the customer is always right, but even when you are trying your best to please the customer and give them what they want, the task of communicating about your shared goal can be challenging.

The term *disambiguation* refers to the process of resolving the conflicts that arise when a single term is ambiguous, and so may refer to more than one topic. As a composer/producer, you will have to clarify any ambiguity in the musical direction you receive from your client.

GENRE OR STYLE ANALYSIS

As a composer/producer, you must research and know the style you are emulating in depth. This can be achieved by study, but most importantly by using your ears.

Every style will have a set of common practice characteristics around several musical elements, which may include:

- Instrumentation
- Form
- Melody
- Chord Progression

- Rhythm
- Tempo
- Vocal
- Influences

Any or all of these may be a defining characteristic of a style.

Let's look at a couple of examples, and how you might fine-tune your understanding and prepare your approach to writing in these styles.

New Orleans Funk

Here's my analysis of New Orleans funk rock:

Instrumentation

Guitar

Electric, but usually not overly distorted.

Drums

Acoustic

Keys

Organ, Rhodes, piano

Horns (sometimes)

Small section

Form

Repeating 4- or 8-bar sections

ABA or AABA song form

Reggae

For comparison, here's my analysis of reggae:

Instrumentation

Guitar

Electric, clean tone

Drums

Acoustic

Timbales

Keys

Organ, Rhodes

Horns

Small section

Form

ABA or AABA song form

(New Orleans Funk)   (Reggae)

Melody   **Melody**

Pentatonic   Pentatonic

Jamaican calypso

Chord Progression   **Chord progression**

Diatonic triads from major and minor   Two-chord vamp in the verse

Dominant 7 vamp   Diatonic triads from major and minor

Rhythm or Pulse   **Rhythm or Pulse**

Sixteenth-note swing   Guitar or keys accent on constant upbeats

Clave   Bass accents beat 2 and 4

Tempo   **Tempo**

Danceable   Slow to moderate

88–108 bpm   80–120 bpm

Vocal   **Vocal timbre**

Predominantly male   Male lead

Unison backgrounds common   Harmony backgrounds

Influences   **Influences**

American funk, James Brown   R&B

Afro/Cuban rhythms, clave   Calypso

French folk melody, Creole, Zydeco   Caribbean

Blues

Rock

My reference for this style is the classic New   My reference here is "Three Little Birds," by
Orleans funk band, the Meters.   Bob Marley.

 "Fire on the Bayou," "Cissy Strut," the Meters
"Three Little Birds," Bob Marley

Note that New Orleans funk and reggae have similar instrumentation, melody, form, vocals, and even some influences, but different rhythmic characteristics. Reggae drives the groove with the constant insistent upbeats. New Orleans funk uses a clave—the "shave and a haircut, two bits" rhythm that crossed over into American pop music from Latin in the hits of Bo Diddley, and Johnny Otis's "Willie and the Hand Jive."

 "Willie and the Hand Jive," Johnny Otis;
"I Shot the Sheriff," Bob Marley

Here's a notation comparison of the two characteristic rhythmic elements.

Reggae   **New Orleans Funk**

FIG. 11.1. Characteristic Rhythmic Elements: Reggae and New Orleans Funk

A great way to see how an arranger might interpret a song in one style into a different style is to listen to this example of a standard gospel ballad as a reggae tune. The verse from Bob Marley's "One Love" is a reggae arrangement of Curtis Mayfield's gospel ballad "People Get Ready."

"People Get Ready," Curtis Mayfield;
"One Love," Bob Marley

As composers and producers doing custom music to someone else's specifications, we want to get it essentially right the first time, or close enough so that reasonable revisions will suffice. This can almost always be achieved with good communication. Often, you can avoid going down the wrong road by singing an idea early in the process, or playing a quick scratch track for the client, even over the phone. Your client will be the final arbiter. Remember that one person's perfume is another person's bug spray. You work for the client—and if you want to keep working, you'll help them realize their vision.

TV PRODUCER'S MUSIC TOOLKIT

A good example of subsequent work stemming from the creation of a television series theme, is the case of a "producer's toolkit." This is a collection of versions in a single genre of the theme in various orchestrations and lengths, along with *stings*—shorter musical clips of various lengths to be used for emphasis, scene transitions, or other subject or mood changes that occur as part of the moving picture editing process.

Case Study: *This Old House* Toolkit

In a couple of cases, the producers of *This Old House* commissioned toolkits in a particular genre to fit a particular series of shows. In the first case, we did a series for the eight episodes chronicling the renovation of "The Bermuda House," Season 25, Episodes 19–26.

TOH Bermuda

The producer/director asked for the song to be arranged in a calypso, or "island" style, with versions that featured steel drums. We had hired acoustic steel drum players for tracks before, but this time, I made the determination that we didn't have the budget to use live drums or live pans. In this case, I called in Tom West, our multitalented keyboardist, composer, and arranger who had worked on literally hundreds of tracks for our studio, to arrange a calypso track using virtual instruments in Logic. I planned to add at least one acoustic instrument for most of the versions. Tom arranged and played keys, virtual bass, virtual drums, and virtual steel drums. I played live acoustic guitar, and edited and mixed in Logic.

Our client referenced the great Sonny Rollins song "St. Thomas," which I was delighted to hear, as it's one of my all-time favorites. As soon as I heard that this was the reference track, I scheduled my friend, the great New Orleans saxophonist Amadee Castenell.

By the way, in an example of failing to prepare properly, when Tom West and I wrote out the sax melody chart, we wrote it in "concert key"—that is, we neglected to write out a transposed part. Since Amadee was not adept at sight transposing (many players are not), the result was that he had to patiently wait around while we scribbled out the melody in the proper key for his instrument. Another good approach would have been to send him an MP3 ahead of time so he could have memorized the part by ear. Either way, our preparation was lacking. Amadee as always played great, though!

30. "TOH Bermuda Sax"
featuring Amadee Castenell

Note that among the main differences between the original melody and the melody in the new arrangements are in the characteristic rhythms of the genre.

When I proudly presented our work to the director, he preferred versions with other lead instruments—flute and "pans" (steel drums)—to that sax version. He may have felt that the sax was too strong a voice, and that it would distract from the narrative of the show. At any rate, I don't think they ever used the sax version. Fortunately, Amadee doubles on flute, and we had the foresight to have him do a flute version as well, which they used!

Here are some tracks that made it to the show. And if you notice that the track length on these examples is unconstrained, you're right! Since they were to be used for scoring episodes and not advertising, there was no need to conform to the usual technical requirements of exact :30 and :60 spots. The director made this clear in his initial directions.

Here is Amadee's flute version.

31. TOH Bermuda Flute

Since we already had the slower tempo track that we had made for the flute, it was relatively easy to create a version with pans in the melody.

32. TOH Bermuda Pans

The next toolkit we did for *This Old House* was at a somewhat higher budget level. I determined that the budget would support live sessions and booked the time at Chris Rival's studio in North Reading, Massachusetts.

Chris is a master of recording live music, using training from his Berklee MP&E degree and his personal aesthetic sense that values heart and soul over technology every time. His studio is large and comfortable to work in, with vintage guitars, amps, and other instruments lining the walls and stacked in the corners.

TOH Country

The idea this time was to go country. Styles to be implemented were western swing and bluegrass.

Here's an email I received from the post-production supervisor at the production company, *This Old House* Productions, Inc. early in the process:

Hi Peter,

Sorry for the delay in getting these notes to you.

Here is the "list" we discussed on 7/8 for TOH music:

- 1 - :60
- a couple of :30 (for variety and fun)
- a couple of stings in the :05–:10 range and in the :25–:35 range

It would be nice to have music for every segue, as well as montages, and a musical transition out of the open.

Some of the descriptions we discussed were: "driving music" (as various people are driving from one location to another, etc.), "freewheeling...swinging" music, and "musical events...to pepper throughout."

David and Gary mentioned isolating some of the instruments, such as the violin, clarinet, and trombone.

Fig. 11.2. Example Post-Production Email

Gary Stephenson was the editor who cut the episodes, and David Vos was the special projects producer/director, who would have final say over the music. I went out to Concord to meet with them to get more detailed direction. They suggested western swing and bluegrass with fiddle, guitar, banjo, and mandolin. This was a vital step. I could have made the mistake of reading the early email and concluding that I needed a trombone player for the session, which was not the case. This is the kind of inadvertent misdirection that often creeps into a process, and it's a good idea to be vigilant about finding out exactly what the decision-maker's vision is in detail.

I called Billy Novick. We discussed the direction and determined that we would go without a drummer. He assembled the players, most notable his partner Guy Van Duser on guitar, who is a world-class fingerstyle, old-time jazz player. Marshall Wood played upright bass, with John Curtis on banjo and mandolin, and the amazing Ian Kennedy on fiddle. Billy played clarinet.

Billy and the others came in well prepared, and the session went smooth as silk. All these players are world class, but Guy blew my mind as always with his unique ability to evoke early swing by playing the guitar like it's an orchestra unto its own.

We did thirty cuts from the session: swing, western swing, bluegrass, even country train style for the "driving music" mentioned by the post-production supervisor, and multiple stings, all done in one day, followed by the two original arrangements for comparison. I recorded a few solo guitar stings myself later.

Note once again that one of the main differences between the original and the new arrangements are in the characteristic rhythms of each genre.

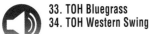

33. TOH Bluegrass
34. TOH Western Swing

For this toolkit, instead of creating the stings by demixing or submixing, for the most part, we recorded them separately. This gave us the opportunity to change the tempo during the sting, starting with energy, and then using a ritardando, gradually slowing to resolve. This is great for an editor who wants to set up a new scene.

Here are a few examples.

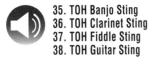

35. TOH Banjo Sting
36. TOH Clarinet Sting
37. TOH Fiddle Sting
38. TOH Guitar Sting

Presentation

Some editors like to have a playlist containing toolkit cuts handy when cutting episodes, both fully arranged versions and stings, with a list of styles, instrumentation, and times.

It's always a good idea to make this list presentable and accurate, and to include your contact info or phone number in case the editor wants to get in touch—for instance, to ask to have a particular edit done that's beyond the scope of their audio editing capability. It's to your advantage to do this kind of editing when asked, or you take the chance of hearing some very awkwardly chopped up version of your music on the air.

In this case, I delivered the tracks on a CD, and listed them clearly on the CD label.

FIG. 11.3. Track Listing for *This Old House* Producer's Toolkit

CHAPTER 12

Getting Paid, Contracts, Agreements, and Industry Practices

MUSIC COPYRIGHT

If the client says, "Make it sound like *popular song X*," how far can you go without getting into trouble?

Association is a very powerful communication tool. It's not unusual for a client to say that they don't know much about music, but they would like their song to sound like a particular song that they know well. As we mentioned, it can be useful for a copywriter to use a well-known song as a template when writing lyrics. Ad industry professionals closely follow current (and past) movies and pop music so that they can try to associate their ad content with popular themes and trends.

Music, like other intellectual property and artistic works, is protected by copyright laws. Even if there is no formal copyright registration, the original recording of a song can be used as a common-law copyright, constituting publication, whatever the format.

The term is currently the author's lifetime plus seventy years. After this period, the work may enter the public domain and no longer be protected. If a song is in the public domain ("PD"), anyone can use it for an advertisement or any other purpose. Otherwise, permission must be granted, and almost always, a licensing fee must be paid. Failure to clear a song by obtaining a license may result in an injunction against use, and/or a lawsuit seeking damages.

To legally establish plagiarism in music, the plaintiff must demonstrate that the defendant not only had access to the plaintiff's song, but also that the two songs are substantially similar, even though some notable elements of music are not subject to protection. The title and the chord progression are not, for instance.

Historically, there have been various ways to define the limits of similarity. The current standard is whether an ordinary listener would, on hearing both songs, judge that one was copied from the other.

One such case involved George Harrison and his song "My Sweet Lord." He was sued on the basis that the song was copied from the Chiffons' "He's So Fine." Note that intent is not a necessary element of infringement. It was generally accepted that the plagiarism was unintentional, but the similarity of the two melodies was so unmistakable that copyright infringement was found, and the plaintiffs were awarded over one and a half million dollars. The quality of the instrumentation, the vocal, and the overall sound are different, but the melody is almost identical.

A contrasting example is the case of Frito-Lay and Tom Waits. Waits was approached with an offer to use his song "Step Right Up" in a radio spot for its product Salsa Rio Doritos tortilla chips. When Waits declined, the spot was made with a song patterned closely on his song, sung by a sound-alike vocalist, Stephen Carter. Waits sued and won an injunction against the use of the song, plus a multi-million dollar settlement. Interestingly, Waits didn't sue for copyright infringement on the basis of plagiarizing the song. Rather, he sued and won for "false endorsement," because the public was deceptively led to believe that he was singing, implying that he was endorsing the product.

In our studio, we have always taken this issue seriously. We always have preferred to work with the desired artist themselves, as you will hear in later examples—for instance, in the cases of Livingston Taylor and the New Kids on the Block. This, of course, is not always possible. In one case, when we were asked to do a BayBank jingle version in the style of Huey Lewis, our arranger/ producer on the job, the talented guitarist and composer Sheldon Mirowitz, cast a vocalist, Chris Farren, who sounded a lot like Lewis. We made sure that the spot aired with an announcement of who in fact was singing. At the top of the spot, there is a prominent VO, "Chris Farren for BayBank."

Direct-to-business clients are sometimes very direct in their requests, whereas agency personnel are usually more familiar with intellectual property rights issues. Imitation is the sincerest form of flattery, but because there are legal limits to how flattering you can be, it's best to avoid a melody that tracks too closely the song you are emulating.

There is another set of problems associated with intellectual property stemming from sampling, the literal reproduction of recorded segments in hip-hop and other genres. There have been some high profile cases and rulings, involving Biz Markie, Vanilla Ice, U2, and Negativland. Suffice it to say, it is not safe to use samples of artists' work without clearing them.

COMMERCIAL MUSIC REVENUE FLOW

Let's trace the path of revenue as it moves through the commercial music industry and estimate the range of revenue potential for each participating entity, including the music house entrepreneur and the composer/producer.

When we estimate a revenue figure, we are referencing the *gross revenue*—the total of all income for the period—not the *net profit* (what's left over after expenses). This is a vital distinction, as gross income can be very high, but if expenses are higher, a business could still lose money. The gross income minus all expenses is the net profit (or "net income"), which is how much money you actually wind up with for the time period.

YouTube does an amazing job of managing an enormous amount of media content. This leads to a high gross revenue amount, received through their placing ads on this content. To put things in perspective, we can look at YouTube as an historical example. In 2011, an average of 35 hours of video were uploaded every minute of every day. These files have to be managed and stored (at no small expense). That year, YouTube claimed that the site had over 700 billion views. Yes, billions. With a B.

YouTube Ad revenue in 2010 doubled over the 2009 numbers, and they did approximately $1.3 billion in gross advertising revenue for the year 2011. Despite the large numbers, the cost of operating and managing the mountain of content to that date was still greater than the income it generated, and YouTube was not yet profitable. In 2015, they were roughly break-even. In 2017, their ad revenue was approximately 3.5 billion dollars and profitability was still uncertain, according to the financial press. High gross revenue is great, but it must exceed expenses in order to generate profits.

As you plan your business activities, you must always keep careful track of expenses. A business may return a varying percentage of total revenue to the bottom line (net profit). Of course, if you're Wal-Mart, then three percent of revenues may constitute 11 billion dollars. In my own experience producing commercial music, 33 percent (about one third of total revenue) is a reasonable figure to set as a goal for net profit on billings. This is much higher than the 10 to 18 percent that most successful small businesses traditionally are expected to realize.

This calculation is completely separate from residual and royalty income, which, if you are lucky enough to earn it, will go straight to the bottom line.

REVENUE BY CLIENT TYPE

Corporate In-House A/V Department

Many large corporations have in-house audio/visual departments that have annual budgets ranging from hundreds of thousands to millions. The originating client in this case is a company that produces their own audio/visual content for use at employee events, investor meetings, conventions, trade shows, or large presentations. Other uses are training or promotional videos, point-of-purchase videos, technology, and product demonstration videos. They may deal directly with vendors and sometimes buy original music from a music house.

As an example, let's look at Assurant Insurance. Assurant is a large insurance company that has claimed 25 billion dollars in assets and an annual revenue of 8 billion dollars. They have A/V departments in multiple cities, each with individual yearly budgets to spend on productions.

A/V Production Company

If a corporate client doesn't have an internal A/V department, they may hire an outside A/V production company that may in turn contract other vendors, including music houses.

Revenues for A/V production companies vary widely according to company size. A sole practitioner may bill one or two hundred thousand dollars a year, while a large A/V company will bill in the millions.

An example of this type of production company is Corporate Audio-Visual Services with offices in Elmsford, New York and Medford, MA. It has a typical annual revenue of at least 1 to 2.5 million dollars.

In my experience, a music house job originating from a corporate in-house production company or an independent A/V production company can be expected to pay the music house in the range of $500 to $5,000 and up. In some cases, way up! ☺

Jobs done directly for A/V departments and companies, commonly referred to as industrials, are one of a music house's "bread and butter" business opportunities. If large, the A/V department or company may be structured like an ad agency with producers, copywriters, creative director. In a smaller organization, many of these roles may be played by just a few individuals.

Production categories of industrials include:

- corporate videos
- industrial videos
- infomercials
- sound-alikes
- slide presentations

Let's consider these in greater detail.

- **Industrial videos**, also known as corporate videos, are long-form videos for many purposes, for instance:
  ○ **a testimonial** or history of the company for an employee gathering.
  ○ **a presentation** for a large gathering of investors.

- **Point-of-purchase promotions** are any media presentations in a store. For an idea of how prevalent this practice is, take a quick look at the Global Association for Marketing at Retail.

- **Infomercials.** Infomercials are broadcast advertisements that may be five minutes or longer. I must admit, I've never been hired to create original music for an infomercial, although I've occasionally heard my library tracks used in them!

- **Sound-alikes.** In the context of corporate music, sound-alikes are usually "knockoffs" of familiar tunes with new lyrics, often celebrating the client company. Among the sound-alikes my studio has done are a version of "Fame" with lyrics rewritten for the company "Bain," and a version of "Celebrate" for Staples at the direction of the founder, Tom Stemberg.

  Because of rights issues, unless a license is obtained from the original artist, these tracks are for use in closed gatherings, not for broadcast or for meetings open to the public. As always, if you're not sure, it's best to consult an intellectual property attorney!

- **Slide Presentations.** When A/V producers have the budget, they may commission musical scores to their slide shows for large events.

Creating music for industrials is an important part of the whole market picture for a music house. It is not the highest paying work you'll do, but it can be a challenging, fun, and over time, a lucrative part of your business.

Music Library

Another source of revenue to the music house, as we have seen, is the music library. In this case, the originating client who purchases music from the library, the buyer, is an individual or corporation that seeks inexpensive music tracks, usually for synchronizing to picture in a video or film.

The buyer may be acting on behalf of themselves, or they may be representing a company or production staff. The buyer may be a local videographer specializing in wedding photography, or any individual creating a video to upload on YouTube. They may be an independent video producer making corporate videos or local spots. They might be an ad agency or television-series producer or documentary filmmaker who wants to use music that, while not custom made, is inexpensive.

An example of this kind of buyer is Bridge Street Productions, of Belmont, MA, owned and operated by Michael Chvany. This one-man video production shop spends $1,500 to $2,500 a year on library music. Michael pays a license fee to the library for downloading and syncing the track, or a subscription fee to the library for unlimited use of a full collection.

Music libraries come in a variety of sizes. One example of a successful library is that of Omnimusic, owned and operated by Doug Wood, with annual revenues of 10 to 20 million dollars.

As we've seen, a music library may pay out a share to the composer/producer, usually in a 50/50 split, or it's possible that the library will have already bought out the rights to the track for a one-time fee.

In the case of a buyout by the library, the composer/producer may receive $10,000 and up for a full album containing ten or more track packages.

In the case of a shared license fee deal on a per download basis, the composer/producer may receive $5 to $100 per download. Depending on the number of track packages the composer has uploaded, and the number of libraries offering the packages, a very prolific composer who has uploaded hundreds of tracks may receive hundreds or even thousands of dollars per month in total.

Advertising Agency

The most lucrative source of work for a music house is the ad agency. The revenue stream originates with the advertiser, who hires one or more ad agencies to craft and manage its advertising. As usual, the range of expenditures is wide.

Nike spends in the billions of dollars a year on advertising. A huge conglomerate such as Proctor and Gamble spends even more a year on advertising.

The stream of revenue from advertisers flows through an ad agency to its vendors, as the agency implements a strategy for a client by creating print and broadcast content. In the case of broadcast radio and television advertising, the agency will hire the vendors necessary to create the content, and then make the appropriate media buys. The agency marks up these expenses (traditionally 15 percent) when it bills the client.

An example of a medium-sized agency is the Boston based agency Hill Holliday, with annual billings in the hundreds of millions as of this writing.

The revenue range for an ad agency is from the low hundreds of thousands for a small shop or sole practitioner, to billions in worldwide billings for the giant conglomerated agencies like BBDO. Agency expenditures for a particular client's campaign may vary from tens of thousands to hundreds of thousands in the case of a local company, to millions of dollars for a regional or national company.

Agency expenditures on a broadcast project can be divided into two categories: the cost of producing the spots and the cost of airing them.

On average, the production of a single 30-second broadcast spot including the film company, actors and actresses, shooting expenses including travel, music, and post-production editing is often in the $350,000 to $500,000 range and sometimes much more. The cost to air the spot may be multiples higher depending on the schedule and number of markets.

The revenue flows from the advertiser who is the originating client, through the agency, to the vendors who participate in the production of the ad content, and to the media where the content is placed. Vendors to ad agencies during the production process include:

- **Casting companies.** The typical gross revenue range per advertising spot job is in the range of thousands to tens of thousands.

- **Film company.** For instance, September Productions in the Boston area. A typical gross revenue range per advertising spot job for a film production company will be tens to hundreds of thousands, or even millions.

- **Post-production video house.** The typical gross revenue range per advertising spot job I would estimate at thousands to tens of thousands.

- **Music house.** We can use Bell Music for an example, with a typical billing range per advertising agency job: $1,500 to $20,000, but with occasional multiple-track projects paying much more.

There is little vendor sub-hiring in the ad agency production market. All the vendors work independently for the agencies, but rarely subcontract to each other. The agency creative team takes responsibility for each component of production and hires the vendors directly.

Once the content is created, the agency makes the media buy. There is a wide range of costs, from thousands to millions, depending on many factors, including how many stations will air the spot, what time the ads play, how often, and in what market or markets. For instance, an ad that plays on local stations late at night will be relatively inexpensive, perhaps even as low as $100 per slot.

The cost of airing a television spot goes up in direct proportion to the number of viewers. If you were to buy a 30-second slot during the Super Bowl, which is seen by possibly 200 million people, the cost is well into the millions.

In the case of themes and scoring for television shows, there are several entities that may be the originating client.

Major Television Studio

The job may originate from a major network television studio, or from the many television production companies that serve the industry.

Backstage, TV Production Companies: Network and Cable

Local Television Studio

Or the originator may be a local station with a production arm such as WGBH Boston for whom we provided theme music to *This Old House, The New Yankee Workshop,* and *Victory Garden.* Another example is Boston area station WCVB for whom we scored a couple of ABC Afterschool movies and provided Emmy-winning music for the public service campaign, "World of Difference."

Other originating clients are the cable networks, such as HBO, and many others, who produce popular series. These entities spend many millions on television production each year. As relates to expenditures on original music, there are a wide range of fees, depending on the size and importance of the project and the reputation of the composer.

A composer's initial revenue for composition, production, and rights to a theme will often be in the range of thousands to tens of thousands of dollars.

Performance Royalties

The composer may realize much more in royalty income, which can reach hundreds of thousands of dollars for a successful show over time. Where does the royalty originate?

Broadcaster networks and cable networks make blanket license payments to the performance rights organizations (PROs): ASCAP, BMI, and SESAC.

As a composer, you must join one of the PROs and list your works with them. The PRO determines when and how its members' music is used, then allots a commensurate share of the blanket payments and sends quarterly payments to members. The tracking of music use is currently undergoing a transformation to digital waveform recognition technology. This will be making tracking significantly more accurate than it has been in the past, when it was based on random listening samples of the airwaves, live performance venues, jukebox plays, and cue sheets submitted by video and film editors or other end users.

A composer whose music is used in a television series as theme and scoring may make performance royalties in the range of thousands to tens of thousands of dollars per year during the life of the show.

Sometimes, an agency will register your work with your PRO for you, but make sure that if they don't, you register the work yourself in order to collect the writer's royalties on your compositions.

CONTRACTS AND OTHER PAPERWORK

Here are some of the types of paperwork you have to manage when you are paying collaborators.

Talent Payments

There are two types of talent payments that are made to performers in all forms of commercial music. The first is a one-time buyout fee paid directly to the performer as an independent contractor. The second is a union session payment, followed by residual payments based on the frequency and market location of broadcast use. These fees vary from hundreds for sessions, to thousands and more for residual payments based on use in many markets and many time cycles.

Tax Forms

If you are doing business in the U.S. and you hire a musician, vocalist, arranger, engineer, or voiceover artist, there are two ways the individual can be paid: as an independent subcontractor or through a union contract. In either case, there is certain information you must collect from your employee. You must have them fill out a W-9 form if they are a subcontractor, or a W-4 form if not. Download these forms at www.irs.gov/forms-instructions.

"Form W-9," www.irs.gov

The forms require the following:

- Full, legal name
- Address
- Social Security number (SSN) or federal tax ID (EIN)

This means that even if you hire someone using a stage name, like the Weeknd (Abel Makkonen Tesfaye), you need their full, current legal name, Social Security number, and address.

Independent Subcontractor

If you hire an independent subcontractor, once you have the signed W-9 form, you will simply pay the individual a fee for services. You must keep careful records of all payments to subcontractor talent. If you pay someone more than $600 total during the year, you will be responsible at the end of the year to send a 1099 form with the exact total to the employee and also send copies to the IRS. This task is reasonably easy to do yourself, or you can involve an outside tax professional to help you.

Full-Time Employees

If you have full-time employees, you will need a completed W-4 form with information listed above, plus the number of withholding allowances claimed.

"Form W-4," www.irs.gov

You will be responsible for paying your full-time employees in accordance with IRS rules relating to withholding and payroll taxes. You also may be responsible for quarterly estimated payments. The taxes usually withheld from employee paychecks include FICA (Medicare and Social Security taxes) and federal, state, and local income taxes. At this point, you should get professional advice from an accountant.

Union Contracts

If an ad agency, television production company, or other client is a *signatory* (i.e., committed to using) to union agreements, then the sessions you conduct for them must include union contracts. The pertinent unions are:

- The American Federation of Musicians (AFM)
- The Screen Actors Guild (SAG)
- The American Federation of Television and Radio Artists (AFTRA)

A union member will get a session fee for performing on the song, and then residual payments. The rates that determine these payments, (union scale) are mandated by the contracts according to the service rendered, the sessions played, how many markets the spot plays in, and how many cycles it plays for.

After each recording session with union players, you (the music house) fill out session contracts, provided by the client or by the local union office, on request. Fill out an AFM contract for instrumentalists and an AFTRA/SAG contract for vocalists. (Agencies typically file directly for voiceover artists.) Your responsibility is to provide the name of each performer and the role they played, and then a copy of the tax form they filled out for you. Ad agencies track and report the usage in each market and use this information to pay associated talent costs to the unions for distribution to the performers as residual payments. Because payments can be quite complicated, agencies typically use a pay service for union payments, such as American Residuals and Talent (ART). This type of company may be colloquially referred to as a "paymaster."

Contract blanks are printed with lots of duplicates in different colors for record keeping by the vendor, the union, the paymaster, and the agency. Each entity has a different contract form for television and radio recording sessions that you can obtain from them if you have an agency job booked.

When doing a union job, all talent must be a current member of the appropriate union, with one exception. Under the Taft-Hartley act, each non-union performer may work one, and only one, union job before being required to be a member. The fee to join AFTRA is currently $3,000. This may sound like a lot, but if a vocalist does a song on an AFTRA contract and the spot plays in more than one market for a number of cycles, the entrance fee will seem relatively low compared to the session and residual compensation realized by the member.

 Taft-Hartley Report

In rare cases, it's possible for a singer to realize hundreds of thousands or even millions of dollars from a national campaign featuring their vocal performances. Sometimes, I wish I had a better singing voice!

Both the entrance fee and the potential residual revenue are much lower for AFM. To join the AFM San Francisco Local 6, for instance, the fee is currently $227.50.

If you play it, arrange it, sing it, or lead it, you will list yourself on the contract. If you think you'll be getting agency or other *signatory work*—work that requires union contracts to be filed—on a regular basis, you should join the AFM or SAG/AFTRA respectively.

Non-Union Jobs

Many potential clients are not union signatories, including most smaller businesses, corporate in-house A/V departments, and video producers. In these cases, you will be hiring talent as independent contractors. This means that you won't be required to withhold taxes or FICA. The contractor is responsible for their own.

Most non-union jobs assume a talent buyout. This means that there will be no residual payments to performers, so this must be part of your negotiated understanding with the talent.

If you don't file a union contract when you hire talent for your productions, you should ask the performer to sign an informal letter of agreement, usually a work-for-hire agreement. This will protect you from misunderstandings and conflicts in the future.

Work for Hire Agreement

Employer: __Bell Music__ Performer: _____

For consideration of creative services and performance (The Work) contributing to the creation of an audio recording project, including all rights in perpetuity to subsequent synchronization, broadcast, advertising or any other use, for the named project or other future projects:

Project name: _____

Fee: $ _____

Producer __Bell Music__ agrees to pay you (Performer) the above amount upon acceptance of The Work.

The Work shall be a work for hire, and Employer shall own the Work, and shall be the sole and exclusive owner of the copyright in The Work, including all rights of copyright registration, renewal and extension. Employer shall also be considered to be the author of The Work for the purposes of U.S. copyright law, and for the purposes of any other applicable state or federal laws. The above Fee will be your sole compensation for The Work.

Employer will have the right to refer to you as a contributing performer in sales and marketing of any Project that includes The Work.

Signature _____ SSN or Federal Tax ID#: _____
            (Performer)

Date: _____

FIG. 12.1. Work-for-Hire Talent Agreement Example

DEMO AND JOB BIDDING

Your bidding strategy will depend on the type of client with whom you are negotiating. All clients are cost-conscious, but the range of music expenditures they are comfortable with can vary widely. The first question I ask a client when the time comes to talk about money is, "What's your budget?" If they are willing to tell you a figure that they have in mind, then you are in good shape. You can calculate your costs for the job as described, and see if you can make a reasonable profit within your client's range.

Video producers, corporate A/V departments, small businesses, and local television producers will have lower budgets in mind than major television producers and ad agencies.

Demo Fees

For a demo, it is understood that the cost will be significantly lower than for a job that has been awarded to be finalized. You are expected to do the demo for a flat fee, "for cost," without making a profit. Some studios have a list-price demo fee in the $1,000 to $5,000 range that doesn't vary. Some studios won't do demos at all, preferring to work only for full price and take a pass on the music-house competitions or other jobs contingent on a demo. Sometimes, it is possible to make a profit on a demo, but the far more important goal is to win the job. Larger agencies are not averse to paying in the thousands for demos, but they won't hesitate to ask for a free demo if their internal budget calls for it.

A composer/producer just starting out must do demos, and do them for the amount offered, even if it's for free. Remember that if you demand a price higher than offered, you may miss out entirely on the job. One hundred percent of nothing is nothing.

Bidding a Commercial Music Job

The basic model for commercial music bidding is called "cost-plus." You estimate a total of your expenses related to the specific job and then add a fee, commonly called a "creative fee." As you do more and more jobs, you will develop a standard creative fee, which may vary widely according to the size of the job, anywhere from $500 to $10,000.

If you can realize economies of scale, or play/sing/arrange on the job, you will personally earn more than the creative fee alone.

After you have gleaned as much information about the job and the budget as you can, you may be asked to submit an itemized bid showing all expenses and fees.

Your bid should include:

- Creative fee.

- Arrangement. Sometimes, this is folded into the creative fee.

- Studio time. Remember to allow ample time for both recording (especially if there are multiple sessions) and mixing.

- Musician session fees.

- Vocal session fees. Even if the musicians' and singers' session fees are paid directly by the agency, as they may be under a union contract, you as the music producer are the expert. The agency may rely on you to estimate these costs.

- Voiceover artist session fees. These may also be covered separately by an agency. If so, these will not be part of your bid.

- Additional or extra expenses, if any (travel, cartage, client services).

Be careful when bidding, because you will be held to your bid when it comes time to bill for a completed job. It's a good idea to ask for a signed bid or work order before you begin, if the job is big enough to warrant it. If your expenses are higher than expected, you must explicitly accept them with the client. You may not need a formal *change order*—a signed work order that changes the scope of the original agreement, in most cases, but if the change is large enough, it's not a bad idea.

Bidding Strategies

For some smaller jobs, you won't need to present an itemized bid to your client. For instance, if you are scoring an industrial video for $2,500, you should estimate your expenses carefully for yourself, but your client may be satisfied with a flat-fee total as a bid. However, when an itemized bid is required, it's important to keep some key points in mind.

- **What do your peers charge?** In general, an ad agency will award you a job on the basis of your ability to deliver the desired creative product, not on the basis of comparative cost—as long as your bid is in a reasonable range determined by common practice. It is worth doing some research to get an idea of common practice in your geographical area. Studios in L.A. and New York generally charge somewhat higher fees than studios in smaller markets. You can call another studio, introduce yourself, then simply describe the job you are bidding and ask for advice. Of course, you are a competitor, so the information may not be forthcoming. In the case of an experienced client like an established ad agency, you can simply ask "What are you used to paying for a job like this?" Once you get a ballpark estimate, you can take it from there, applying what you now know of common practice to your own specific estimated expenses and creative fee calculation.

- **What have you charged in the past for similar work?** The range of fees that you charge will become part of the identity of your service. Once clients have an expectation of what you'll do a job for, they won't like to be surprised by your next bid. Strive for consistency.

- **What is in the agency's budget for music?** A larger agency generally has the resources to afford to pay higher fees. This is contingent on the size and resources of their client. If they offer more than you are used to getting, by all means accept. However, don't simply assume that you will get more for a job from a bigger agency or client. You don't want the agency to think that their smaller competitors are getting your services for less. Once again, strive for consistency.

- **What are your projected costs?** Your costs will vary. If you play all the parts on an instrumental track by yourself, using virtual instruments on your laptop, your job-specific, out-of-pocket talent expenses are zero. If the job calls for itemized expenses, however, you are entitled to pay yourself a session fee for each part you program or play, just as though you had hired someone else. This can get out of hand easily, though. I don't recommend claiming to your client that a loop of a cowbell part deserves a separate session fee.

If you are hiring vocalists and musicians, there are two basic standards.

1. The first is the going rate in your area for a musician or vocalist for a three-hour recording session. This may vary according to how much demand the performer is in, but most performers will work for the going rate. The rate for most players in my area hasn't changed much in the last twenty years: it is in the $200 to $400 range for a three-hour session. For a vocalist, it's a bit higher: in the $250 to $400 range for a lead singer.

2. The second standard is derived from the AFM and AFTRA rates. As mentioned earlier, a client that is a signatory will handle all residual payments but may want you to include the session fees in your bid. For current rates, check the union sites, or give them a call and include an accurate estimate using the AFM commercials rate. For AFTRA, the session rate is per song or per hour—whichever is greater. For a lead or duet vocal, it is one rate; for a group of three or more, a different rate per vocalist. Keep in mind that union-scale rates can get very complicated. When in doubt, consult a union representative.

If you are hiring an outside studio with an engineer, you will pay in the range of one hundred to several hundred dollars an hour. Simply calculate how many hours you will need to record basics, solos, voiceovers, vocals, horns, strings, and then mix.

If you are using your own studio, and acting as your own engineer, even if it is in your dining room, you are entitled to charge an hourly rate per job. This is legitimate, to offset your fixed costs for purchasing and maintaining the studio space and gear, including your computer.

You will also be responsible for sales tax, if your state requires it. Don't forget to charge it and to pay it. Your clients will be used to seeing it as part of the bill. My business went through a sales tax audit years ago. Luckily, we were in compliance!

Terms

Cash flow is an important issue for a music producer. You must be able to pay your talent on the spot for demos and non-union contract jobs. It is reasonable to ask for money up front to cover production expenses (often fifty percent). This can be billed separately as a deposit. It is also reasonable to ask that the balance be paid in full within thirty days of delivery ("net 30"). Most agencies will take longer to pay the balance (often ninety days), but it's common practice to ask that the deposit be paid before work starts.

Fine-Tuning a Bid

If it looks like the budgeted amount won't cover the studio and session fees for the number of musicians you were hoping to use, you can either change the number of musicians or offer each musician a lower fee. Finally, you can adjust your creative fee. You can calculate this in your head or with a calculator. A great way to do it is with a spreadsheet program where totals are a function of other variables and can be changed at will.

Make sure you organize the bid to include:

- job description
- deliverables
- studio time
- talent costs

- arranging fees
- creative fee
- sub-totals, (tax) and total
- payment terms

BELL MUSIC

43 Hillside Road
Watertown, MA 02472

Voice: 617-923-7700
peterbellmusic.com

To: *Name* _____ *Date* _____
   Company _____
   Address _____
   _____

Proposal: _____

Compose and produce one <u>:30 TV Donut Jingle</u> _____

Title: <u>*Composition*</u> _____

Arrangement 1			5 Rhythm/Male Lead/3 Backs/4 Horns	
Vocals				
Lead Vocal	*	1	@ 300	300
Background vocal	*	3	@ 250	750
Rhythm Section				
Drums				
Bass				
Guitar 1				
Guitar 2				
Keys	*	5	@ 200	1,000
Horns				
Brass/Reeds	*	4	@ 200	800
Studio				
Basics	*	4	@ 80	320
Horns	*	1		80
Vocals	*	2		160
Solos, Sweetening, Overdubbing	*	2		160
Mix and Stem	4	*		320
Arrangement	*	*		500
Arr 1 Subtotal:				4,390
Creative Fee:				<u>5,000</u>

Total: $9,390

Terms: 50% on acceptance, balance on delivery net 30

Signed: _____   _____
            (for Bell Music)   (for Agency)

FIG. 12.2. Bell Music Bid Proposal

CHAPTER 13

Hits, PSAs, Agency Pitches, and the Ones That Got Away

POP MUSIC AND REMAKES IN ADVERTISING

We started this book by describing a time when advertising music was for the most part distinct from pop music. We mentioned exceptions, like the Coke song, "I'd Like to Teach the World to Sing" in 1971, which became a pop hit after being a song. Another exception was the Ray Charles Pepsi campaign, which brought legitimacy and star power to ad music. This blurred the lines but didn't erase them, as the music was created for ads, not for pop music airplay.

To paraphrase online pop culture commentator Carrie McLaren: Early advertising music was primarily used as a mnemonic device. Rhyme and repetition were enlisted in jingles for memorability. Music now is more often employed as "borrowed interest" that conveys an atmosphere, sets a mood, or recalls past experiences.

Beginning in 1985, with Nike licensing the Beatles "Revolution," the floodgates gradually broke. In 1991, Chevy started using "Like a Rock" by Bob Seger, and found it so effective that it continued the practice until 2004. In 1995, Microsoft paid millions to use the Rolling Stones hit "Start Me Up" in spots. Subsequently, many of the musicians of the '60s and '70s, whose music and lyrics eschewed commercialism and were steeped in idealism, allowed their music to be used in advertising, joining the ranks of artists of other eras who felt comfortable with the practice.

"Chevy, Like a Rock"

There are notable holdouts. As mentioned, Tom Waits refuses to let his music be used in advertising, or even a likeness of his voice. He is adamant in his disapproval of the practice. Bonnie Raitt will do PSAs, as in the American Red Cross Blood Drive voiceover she did for my studio, but she will not license her music for advertising.

Bob Dylan, perhaps the epitome of '60s social upheaval and alienation, now is heard on ads for Cadillac, Victoria's Secret, and Pepsi with will.i.am.

Pepsi "Forever Young" featuring
Bob Dylan and will.i.am

The practice of "borrowing interest" has evolved beyond the use of using hits to creating ads with pop music stars in a variety of roles, implying their endorsement of the product. As far back as the 2010 Super Bowl, a number of ads of this type aired, featuring musical performance and/or acting by recording artists including Kiss for Dr. Pepper, Beyoncé for Vizio, Stevie Wonder for Volkswagen, and T-Pain for Bud Light, among others.

Another example, of course, of pop stars participating in advertising is that of the New Kids on the Block singing our BayBank song for my studio. The New Kids certainly didn't need the relatively modest amount of money that they received for the spot. That year, they earned many tens of millions of dollars in their pop career. The reason they decided to participate is that, being from Dorchester (a neighborhood of Boston), they were gung-ho to be a part of Boston culture, and by then, the BayBank song had become just that.

There is no statute of limitations on pop music in advertising, when it comes to bringing back hits from past. Here's an example of an ad that reaches back many decades for "borrowed interest."

AT&T Blackberry Torch
"Rollercoaster," Buddy Holly
"Every Day" Remakes

Remakes

A second strategy is to license a popular song but instead of using the hit version, to cover the song with a different performance. An example is the 2011 spot for Mio with a cover of the KC and the Sunshine Band classic 1975 disco hit "That's the Way I Like It."

Kraft MIO,
"Add a Little or Lot"

A different method that may occasionally catch the imagination of agency creatives is to license a known song, and then produce it afresh using completely different lyrics derived from a particular campaign strategy and tagline. The reason for this is obvious: copywriters will imagine a song using music they are familiar with as a reference. If it's affordable and works well enough, it follows that the reference song can be licensed and repurposed for advertising. The idea is that if the copywriter easily makes the association, then the audience will too.

A perfect example of this is the UPS Logistics campaign, using the song "That's Amore" from the '50s. This campaign is effective enough that it's worth taking a close look at what they have done with a classic song with new words.

"That's Amore," by Harry
Warren and Jack Brooks 1953,
performed by Dean Martin

The UPS version of the song is sung with lyrics from the campaign written by the ad agency Ogilvy and Mather. The title lyric/hook, "That's Amore," is swapped for the tagline "That's Logistics."

"That's Logistics" lyrics,
"That's Logistics :30" and/or
"That's Logistics :60"

What we can now call "the UPS Logistics song" features the cute playful voice of Australian Nadia Ackerman. Her accent is for the most part well disguised but comes through subtly in a couple of spots.

Here is a fascinating description of the UPS strategic thinking regarding the campaign.

Inside the UPS "That's Logistics" Campaign

In an example of subsequent work related to the UPS Logistics song, the agency created a spot in which the melody is played by a rock guitar. Of course, this never would have had the "logistics" association without being preceded by the full sing version enough times that when we hear the melody, we no longer think "That's Amore," but now think "That's Logistics."

There are numerous other examples of repurposing a pop song for advertising. Check *Adweek* for a compilation of the fifty top songs used in commercials.

One fun example is the satirical transformation of Helen Reddy's "I Am Woman" into a spot for Burger King entitled "I Am Man" done by the agency Crispin Porter Bogusky.

"I Am Man," Burger King

If this type of work is offered to you, keep in mind that the ad agency will be responsible for licensing the song for the use of their client. Make sure that it's been done. If not, you can contact the PROs yourself. They are there to help. You can even search a particular song on ASCAP and BMI online for rights holders. Without that license, you are liable!

PUBLIC SERVICE ANNOUNCEMENTS (PSAS)

Music houses sometimes receive requests to do music for public service announcement (PSA) campaigns. Usually, this is work that we do for free, although sometimes an agency will offer to cover expenses. Of course, you don't have to contribute your talent for free if you don't want to. But doing pro bono work on PSAs is not just personally rewarding, it's good for business. You will build your relationship with your client around teaming up together to do something worthwhile.

American Red Cross

One PSA my studio did was for the "Give Blood" campaign for the American Red Cross. For this campaign, we made numerous arrangements of the jazz standard song "Makin' Whoopee," by Walter Donaldson and Gus Kahn. The message is that when you give blood, you help prolong a life and make the celebration of new important life experiences possible by providing another season, another reason, for makin' whoopee, etc., etc.

Here's one of the beds we created: an arrangement using fretless bass and whistled melody:

39. Red Cross "Makin' Whoopee"
    Whistle

Here's another one of the arrangements, improvised for us by the great jazz guitarist, Mick Goodrick. This track and others were then used as beds for cameo voiceovers by well-known stars such as Randy Travis and Bonnie Raitt, among others.

40. Red Cross "Makin' Whoopee"
    Solo Guitar, by Mick Goodrick

In this next spot, we were lucky enough to work with Layla Hathaway, who scatted the song so beautifully while the message was delivered by simple on-screen lettering. She is one of the premier jazz vocalists of our time and was very generous to lend her talent and super positive energy to the project.

41. Red Cross "Makin' Whoopee"
    Scat, Layla Hathaway

In the next example, I played acoustic, Paul Rishell played slide, and Bonnie Raitt provided the star voiceover.

42. Red Cross "Give Blood,"
    Bonnie Raitt

A World of Difference

Another campaign that we worked on was the *Make a World of Difference* series. This was Boston TV station WCVB's campaign to promote tolerance and inclusion.

My strategy was to create a memorable melody based on two consecutive intervals of a perfect fourth (Sol, Do, Fa) followed by a pentatonic resolution (Sol, La, Do). We produced the track with a flute lead, played by Matt Marvuglio. We were happy to be a part of a good cause, and we won an Emmy for our efforts.

As the campaign was revived after some years, we ended up doing arrangements in several styles.

I hope they bring the campaign back again. I'd love to do more arrangements and support a cause that will always be relevant. Here's one of my favorites of the versions we did, arranged by Chris Parks.

43. World of Difference :30

THE AGENCY NEW BUSINESS PITCH

Music houses are often part of the frantic activity that accompanies a competitive pitch on the part of the agency where it vies with other agencies for the business of an important client. This is the frenetic, high-intensity agency new business pitch. Each agency creates and presents a "virtual" campaign, usually including mock TV and radio ads, and it may involve vendors to develop this content for presentation to the client. You may be asked to participate gratis, or for expenses only. You should jump at the chance to bond with the agency, and if they win, although there is no guarantee, they will usually include you in the resulting production work. Many times, the pitch campaign is not the one that gets produced for broadcast, even if it wins the job for the agency.

One such case involving our studio was that of the Mullen Advertising/ Veryfine pitch. Known for cutting-edge creative, led by their brilliant creative director Edward Boches, Mullen was vying for the Veryfine Juice account. I suggested that they present a version with new lyrics of the classic Fiestas hit, "So Fine," written by Johnny Otis.

"So Fine," the Siestas

We did a number of versions for the pitch, including this one, featuring the super talented, and now-famous Grammy Award winning singer/songwriter Patty Griffin.

44. "So Fine" Patty

We then produced a series using a more pop/rock arrangement, with three of our best steady jingle singers: Cecilia Cavicchio, Mike Payette, and Darcel Wilson. Finally, we offered up two more arrangements, the first with the a capella group, No Visible Means of Support. Our final effort was a quirky arrangement featuring the clever and talented Chic Street Man.

45. "So Fine" Cecilia
46. "So Fine" Mike
47. "So Fine" Darcel
48. "So Fine" No Visible Means of Support
49. "So Fine" Chic

I was very happy and excited about the tracks we provided, and Mullen did win the account. We were glad to have participated, and we benefited by getting further work from Mullen subsequently.

THE ONES THAT GOT AWAY

No matter how hard you work in the commercial music business, it is a fact of life that some of your best work will go unappreciated. With no disrespect intended to the client, there will be times when your audience simply doesn't understand or appreciate the quality of a creative idea or a music track even when it's great. Just because your client (or their client) doesn't appreciate the value of the work doesn't mean it isn't valuable, though.

Repurposing

Repurposing is a general term that may describe the practice of using a pop song in advertising or creating a sound-alike with new lyrics. It may describe another common practice in the industry: to use a rejected track for a different project. Make sure that the original client that rejected your track is okay with the track being used for another client.

Agencies are fiercely competitive with each other. An important creative team employee at an agency will often sign a *non-disclosure agreement* (also known as a "confidentiality agreement"—a legal contract between parties to restrict access to information by third parties) and or a *non-compete agreement* (one party, usually an employee, agrees not to pursue a similar profession or trade in competition against another party, usually the employer) as part of their employment contracts. These contracts prevent the employee from sharing information with competitors, and in some cases, even from accepting employment from competitors if the employee leaves the agency.

There are also specific contractual agreements that may come into play for the track or tracks in question. The agency may have secured rights to the music contractually when they hired you. Even if that's not the case, they will usually rightly feel that they have a stake in the creative process that produced the tracks. Although there is widespread poaching of ideas between ad agencies, agency creative teams regard their ideas as proprietary, whether they are legally protected or not.

Occasionally, our studio has reused a rejected song idea for another client. However, for the most part, our practice has been, when repurposing, not to reuse an unused or rejected track for a rival agency, but to develop it into a music library track package.

Here's an example of a song developed in a pitch for Ocean Spray Hawaiian Punch that wasn't used. At the direction of the agency, our production was already a remake version of the 1940 Mills Brothers hit, "Java Jive," with altered lyrics.

**50. Ocean Spray
:30 Big D**

I really liked this track, with "Big D" on vocal and Larry Carsman on slide guitar. When I remade the track, I wanted to steer clear of copyright infringement. I used a similar progression, with a different melody. I created a track package with the usual :15, :30, :60, full mix, and alt mix. I played all the parts myself. For the bass, I used an acoustic bass patch in Logic. Since I don't own, or know how to play, a ukulele, I used a child size nylon string guitar I bought for my daughter when she was little. For the slide, I used my Strat, in open tuning. I'm not nearly as good at slide as Larry is, to say the least, but through the miracle of Logic's editing features, I made it work well enough, I think. ☺

51. "Maui Waui" :60

The moral is, always archive everything you do. Never throw away a track or even an idea. A use may come along for it, and when it does, you'll be glad you didn't discard it. As you archive these tracks, keep a record of the original purpose and the full brief so you can easily find what you're looking for at a later date. I keep a folder with unsold tracks and their original sessions just in case a new possible use occurs to me.

AWARDS/TRADE MAGAZINES

Every year, the trade organizations of the advertising community honor their picks for the best in broadcast advertising. There are a number of different awards that a music house can compete for. Usually, the agencies are aggressive about submitting their work, and if your track is a part of a spot that wins, you'll get some recognition. There are some awards that are specifically for music, and those are the ones that are most important to the reputation of a music house.

Every market has award shows geared to the ad agency creative community.

You should check your geographical area for available awards, and submit your work when you think it is worthy. There is usually a fee for submission, so pick carefully. When you have done great work, you should lobby the agency to submit it to the shows. When it wins, you both benefit. As usual, the best work doesn't always win!

The Emmy awards have been given since 1949 for excellence in television production by the Academy of Television Arts & Sciences. The awards are given nationally and regionally. My studio has been lucky enough to win twice at the New England regional level. We were fortunate to win a number of New England Broadcast Association (NEBA) awards as well.

Other honors are awarded by the trade magazines. Trade magazines are a treasure trove of information for a music house. They are your best resource for defining and researching the advertising agency world.

Some prominent advertising trade magazines are:

- *Adweek*, founded in 1978. Of special interest, currently, is the entertaining and informative *AdFreak* blog from this organization.

- *Advertising Age*, since 1930, delivering news, analysis, and data on marketing and media. They too have a terrific site, Creativity, which showcases the latest TV spots and campaigns with full production credits and reviews.

- *Backstage* is a trade magazine for people working in the entertainment industry, including advertising. It is a good resource for information concerning the performance unions, SAG, AFTRA, and the AFM.

Bell Music's awards list includes:

- 2 Emmy awards

- 7 NEBA awards

- 10 ASCAP awards

- 1 Backstage Top 10 Madison Ave Singles award

Winning awards will not guarantee success, but they certainly help your reputation within the ad community. Any recognition that you can get for your work will help open doors and give you an opportunity to compete for ad agency work.

The Artist vs. the Journeyman

What is art? I'd have to say that advertising technically fits my definition: art is creative work using any medium, whether physical, visual, or auditory, to express a concept or feeling.

However, we instinctively make a distinction between art made for the love of making it and art made for financial gain. So, in this sense, we may make a distinction between an *artist*, whose only desire is to express himself, and a *craftsman*, who is creating a work to someone else's vision. However, this distinction has historically been blurred by the artists' need to support themselves.

What is art worth? Nothing brings home the truth that beauty is in the eye of the beholder so much as the fact that nineteenth-century painter Vincent Van Gogh's paintings now sell for millions of dollars, but he died penniless at thirty-seven without ever selling a single painting outside his family.

Is making commercial music selling out? Is there a limit to what you will do as a commercial musician? Would you make music for a cigarette ad? For a political campaign that you didn't agree with?

As commercial music composers, are we artists or *journeymen* (a craftsman or tradesperson)? Does journeyman work deserve respect? Do musicians compromise their integrity, morality, or principles in exchange for money or success when they create music for advertising?

Some, like Tom Waits, feel that advertising is not a valid endeavor for an artist. Others, like Andrew Bird, have legitimate status as artists but may be happy to benefit from the exposure of their music to a wide audience through use in advertising. Some very successful pop artists, such as Ray Charles, Stevie Wonder, and the Rolling Stones, don't really need more money or exposure, but have lent their talents to advertising, perhaps because they like being a part of the broad culture. Many of us are just trying to make a living making music—and hopefully, without doing harm.

In the final analysis, these are the type of questions that musicians have to answer for themselves.

GLOSSARY

:15, :30, :60	common radio or TV spot lengths, in seconds, often used to refer to a particular version of a track
agency creative team	usually art director, agency producer, copywriter
alt mix	a stereo mixdown without some multitrack elements or with altered elements
bed	see *music bed*
bespoke	made to order according to specified direction
bounce	render a mix or individual audio file to disk, from a DAW
brand	company or product identity
brief	an outline of the parameters of a commercial music job, furnished to the music composer/producer by the ad agency or direct client
bumper, button	short musical segment used in transitions, especially into or out of a commercial break (also "sting")
buyout	purchase of all rights to intellectual property, including royalty rights
campaign	integrated marketing plan and strategy for promotion of a product, including branding, using all media—especially broadcast and print advertising content
campaign song	jingle
copy	text of advertising content, especially the VO
crowdsourcing	obtaining content for resale by soliciting contributions from the online community
cue	a specific musical element to fit a specific scene
cut	*verb:* to edit video *noun:* a particular video edit of a spot
DAW	digital audio workstation: sequencing, recording, and editing software used to produce music
donut	a jingle with a sing at the top, an instrumental music bed section for a voiceover, and a tag sing at the tail
editor	video or film editor who creates the finished TV or film edit from the raw footage
full mix	an all-inclusive multitrack to stereo mix of any production
full sing	a jingle with lyrics sung throughout, often including verse, chorus, and tag
hit point	a specific screen action or scene change used as a sync point for a musical event or change in the score
jingle	a song written with the express purpose of promoting a brand or product on broadcast TV, radio, Web, point of purchase, or any other method of publication that contains audio
music bed	an instrumental track used as background for picture or VO narration (also "bed")
music supervisor	the person in charge of the music for a film or TV show

pitch	a sales presentation, in particular, to or by an advertising agency
points	shorthand for payment terms tied to a percentage; short for percentage points
post-production, post	TV or film term for all stages of production occurring after shooting or recording initial material, during which video editors lay back audio elements to the picture along with voiceover, narration, and ambient audio in a mix-to-pix session at a studio designed for that purpose before publishing or broadcast
PRO	performance rights organization (ASCAP, BMI, SESAC)
promos	broadcast spot promotions for a radio or TV show
PSA	public service announcement
public service announcement	an advertisement created for a charitable cause or in the public interest
radio ID jingles	a short vocal jingle comprised of the call-letters of a radio station
residuals	union-required payments beyond the initial session fee, tied to use of the spot or film over time, and in particular markets
ringtones	short lo-fi samples used in cell phones to signal calls; these are sometimes a loop taken from a familiar song
rough mix	an unfinished bounced stereo mix of the current state of the music (also "ruff")
royalties	income stream to rights holders collected by PROs for the public performance of music
ruff	see *rough mix*
SAG/AFTRA	Screen Actors Guild/American Federation of Television and Radio Actors; performer and media professional union
score	music under the dramatic action of TV or film not scripted or sourced, technically termed "incidental music" (also "underscore")
sound design	a score that includes or features sound effects, musical and otherwise
sound effects	sounds recorded naturally or created artificially to enhance a production
soundtrack	the sound for a movie, video, infomercial, or advertisement, which may include music, effects, dialogue, voiceover, and any other audio elements.
source music	music used in a film or TV show with a scripted source in the scene (for instance a radio)
spot	any radio or television advertisement
spotting, spotting session	meeting between composer and director for analyzing film or video to discuss and identify placement of cues, sound effects, and musical articulations in a score, and to specify hit-points
stems	individually bounced audio files of tracks of a multitrack recording
sting	see bumper, button
storyboard	a series of illustrations providing a representation of the finished television commercial in a sequence of scenes; includes text descriptions and dialog
tag, tagline	a slogan, often sung or spoken at the end of a spot
underscore	see *score*
VO	voiceover
voiceover	narration
work-for-hire	a buyout of intellectual property or service including copyright or musical performance

INDEX

ABOUT THE AUTHOR

Peter Bell, Electronic Music and Production faculty at Berklee College of Music, is a producer, composer, and guitarist. His commercial music compositions and productions include the themes to *This Old House, New Yankee Workshop, Victory Garden,* the *ABC After School Special,* the award-winning film *Radio Cape Cod,* and countless jingles and production tracks. Peter has produced tracks featuring many world-class musicians, including Livingston Taylor, Kate Taylor, Alex Taylor, Ray Greene, Rory Block, John Poussette-Dart, the New Kids on the Block, Tracey Bonham, Layla Hathaway, Rebecca Parris, Mick Goodrick, Mark Sandman (of Morphine), Patty Griffin, Bonnie Raitt, and many others.

Photo by Jonathan Feist

Peter's guitar performance credits include Bonnie Raitt, Susan Tedeschi, Kate Taylor, and James Montgomery. He has recorded with Bonnie Raitt on Warner Brothers, and the James Montgomery Band on Capricorn and Island Records. His awards include two Emmys, seven NEBA awards, and six ASCAP awards. Peter holds a bachelor of music in jazz composition and arranging from Berklee College of Music and a BA in government from Harvard.

Peter is currently producing his own music and others' along with long-time collaborator David Mash under the name Bar of 2 Productions (visit www.barof2.com).

More Fine Publications

Berklee Press

GUITAR

BEBOP GUITAR SOLOS
by Michael Kaplan
00121703 Book.............................$16.99

BLUES GUITAR TECHNIQUE
by Michael Williams
50449623 Book/Online Audio...........$24.99

BERKLEE GUITAR CHORD DICTIONARY
by Rick Peckham
50449546 Jazz – Book.........................$12.99
50449596 Rock – Book.........................$12.99

BERKLEE GUITAR STYLE STUDIES
by Jim Kelly
00200377 Book/Online Media..........$24.99

CLASSICAL TECHNIQUE FOR THE MODERN GUITARIST
by Kim Perlak
00148781 Book/Online Audio.............$19.99

CONTEMPORARY JAZZ GUITAR SOLOS
by Michael Kaplan
00143596 ....$16.99

CREATIVE CHORDAL HARMONY FOR GUITAR
by Mick Goodrick and Tim Miller
50449613 Book/Online Audio.............$19.99

FUNK/R&B GUITAR
by Thaddeus Hogarth
50449569 Book/Online Audio $19.99

GUITAR CHOP SHOP – BUILDING ROCK/METAL TECHNIQUE
by Joe Stump
50449601 Book/Online Audio............$19.99

GUITAR SWEEP PICKING
by Joe Stump
00151223 Book/Online Audio.............$19.99

INTRODUCTION TO JAZZ GUITAR
by Jane Miller
00125041 Book/Online Audio $19.99

JAZZ GUITAR FRETBOARD NAVIGATION
by Mark White
00154107 Book/Online Audio $19.99

JAZZ SWING GUITAR
by Jon Wheatley
00139935 Book/Online Audio.............$19.99

A MODERN METHOD FOR GUITAR*
by William Leavitt
Volume 1: Beginner
00137387 Book/Online Video............$24.99
*Other volumes, media options, and supporting songbooks available.

A MODERN METHOD FOR GUITAR SCALES
by Larry Baione
00199318 Book.............................$10.99

Berklee Press publications feature material developed at the Berklee College of Music.
To browse the complete Berklee Press Catalog, go to
www.berkleepress.com

BASS

BASS LINES
Fingerstyle Funk
by Joe Santerre
50449542 Book/Online Audio $19.95
Metal
by David Marvuglio
00122465 Book/Online Audio.............$19.99
Rock
by Joe Santerre
50449478 Book/CD $19.95

BERKLEE JAZZ BASS
by Rich Appleman, Whit Browne, and Bruce Gertz
50449636 Book/Online Audio $19.99

FUNK BASS FILLS
by Anthony Vitti
50449608 Book/Online Audio...........$19.99

INSTANT BASS
by Danny Morris
50449502 Book/CD $9.99

VOICE

BELTING
by Jeannie Gagné
00124984 Book/Online Media............$19.99

THE CONTEMPORARY SINGER – 2ND ED.
by Anne Peckham
50449595 Book/Online Audio $24.99

JAZZ VOCAL IMPROVISATION
by Mili Bermejo
00159290 Book/Online Audio $19.99

TIPS FOR SINGERS
by Carolyn Wilkins
50449557 Book/CD..............................$19.95

VOCAL TECHNIQUE
featuring Anne Peckham
50448038 DVD....................................$19.95

VOCAL WORKOUTS FOR THE CONTEMPORARY SINGER
by Anne Peckham
50448044 Book/Online Audio..........$24.99

YOUR SINGING VOICE
by Jeannie Gagné
50449619 Book/Online Audio $29.99

WOODWINDS/BRASS

TRUMPET SOUND EFFECTS
by Craig Pederson & Ueli Dörig
00121626 Book/Online Audio.............$14.99

SAXOPHONE SOUND EFFECTS
by Ueli Dörig
50449628 Book/Online Audio $15.99

THE TECHNIQUE OF THE FLUTE: CHORD STUDIES, RHYTHM STUDIES
by Joseph Viola
00214012 Book..$19.99

PIANO/KEYBOARD

BERKLEE JAZZ KEYBOARD HARMONY
by Suzanna Sifter
00138874 Book/Online Audio...........$24.99

BERKLEE JAZZ PIANO
by Ray Santisi
50448047 Book/Online Audio $19.99

BERKLEE JAZZ STANDARDS FOR SOLO PIANO
Arranged by Robert Christopherson, Hey Rim Jeon, Ross Ramsay, Tim Ray
00160482 Book/Online Audio...........$19.99

CHORD-SCALE IMPROVISATION FOR KEYBOARD
by Ross Ramsay
50449597 Book/CD.................................$19.99

CONTEMPORARY PIANO TECHNIQUE
by Stephany Tiernan
50449545 Book/DVD $29.99

HAMMOND ORGAN COMPLETE
by Dave Limina
50449479 Book/CD $24.99

JAZZ PIANO COMPING
by Suzanne Davis
50449614 Book/Online Audio $19.99

LATIN JAZZ PIANO IMPROVISATION
by Rebecca Cline
50449649 Book/Online Audio..........$24.99

SOLO JAZZ PIANO – 2ND ED.
by Neil Olmstead
50449641 Book/Online Audio...........$39.99

DRUMS

BEGINNING DJEMBE
by Michael Markus & Joe Galeota
00148210 Book/Online Video $16.99

BERKLEE JAZZ DRUMS
by Casey Scheuerell
50449612 Book/Online Audio.............$19.99

DRUM SET WARM-UPS
by Rod Morgenstein
50449465 Book....................................$12.99

A MANUAL FOR THE MODERN DRUMMER
by Alan Dawson & Don DeMichael
50449560 Book.......................................$14.99

MASTERING THE ART OF BRUSHES – 2ND EDITION
by Jon Hazilla
50449459 Book/Online Audio...........$19.99

PHRASING: ADVANCED RUDIMENTS FOR CREATIVE DRUMMING
by Russ Gold
00120209 Book/Online Media............$19.99

WORLD JAZZ DRUMMING
by Mark Walker
50449568 Book/CD $22.99

STRINGS/ROOTS MUSIC

BERKLEE HARP
Chords, Styles, and Improvisation for Pedal and Lever Harp
by Felice Pomeranz
00144263 Book/Online Audio $19.99

BEYOND BLUEGRASS
Beyond Bluegrass Banjo
by Dave Hollander and Matt Glaser
50449610 Book/CD $19.99

Beyond Bluegrass Mandolin
by John McGann and Matt Glaser
50449609 Book/CD $19.99

Bluegrass Fiddle and Beyond
by Matt Glaser
50449602 Book/CD $19.99

EXPLORING CLASSICAL MANDOLIN
by August Watters
00125040 Book/Online Media $19.99

THE IRISH CELLO BOOK
by Liz Davis Maxfield
50449652 Book/Online Audio $24.99

JAZZ UKULELE
by Abe Lagrimas, Jr.
00121624 Book/Online Audio $19.99

BERKLEE PRACTICE METHOD

GET YOUR BAND TOGETHER
With additional volumes for other instruments, plus a teacher's guide.
Bass
by Rich Appleman, John Repucci and the Berklee Faculty
50449427 Book/CD $16.99
Drum Set
by Ron Savage, Casey Scheuerell and the Berklee Faculty
50449429 Book/CD $14.95
Guitar
by Larry Baione and the Berklee Faculty
50449426 Book/CD $16.99
Keyboard
by Russell Hoffmann, Paul Schmeling and the Berklee Faculty
50449428 Book/Online Audio $14.99

WELLNESS

MANAGE YOUR STRESS AND PAIN THROUGH MUSIC
by Dr. Suzanne B. Hanser and Dr. Susan E. Mandel
50449592 Book/CD $29.99

MUSICIAN'S YOGA
by Mia Olson
50449587 Book $17.99

THE NEW MUSIC THERAPIST'S HANDBOOK – 3RD EDITION
by Dr. Suzanne B. Hanser
00279325 Book................................... $29.99

AUTOBIOGRAPHY

LEARNING TO LISTEN: THE JAZZ JOURNEY OF GARY BURTON
by Gary Burton
00117798 Book $27.99

MUSIC THEORY/EAR TRAINING/ IMPROVISATION

BEGINNING EAR TRAINING
by Gilson Schachnik
50449548 Book/Online Audio $16.99

THE BERKLEE BOOK OF JAZZ HARMONY
by Joe Mulholland & Tom Hojnacki
00113755 Book/Online Audio........... $27.50

BERKLEE MUSIC THEORY – 2ND ED.
by Paul Schmeling
Rhythm, Scales Intervals
50449615 Book/Online Audio $24.99
Harmony
50449616 Book/Online Audio $22.99

IMPROVISATION FOR CLASSICAL MUSICIANS
by Eugene Friesen with Wendy M. Friesen
50449637 Book/CD $24.99

REHARMONIZATION TECHNIQUES
by Randy Felts
50449496 Book $29.99

MUSIC BUSINESS

ENGAGING THE CONCERT AUDIENCE
by David Wallace
00244532 Book/Online Media $16.99

HOW TO GET A JOB IN THE MUSIC INDUSTRY – 3RD EDITION
by Keith Hatschek with Breanne Beseda
00130699 Book.................................... $27.99

MAKING MUSIC MAKE MONEY
by Eric Beall
50448009 Book $27.99

MUSIC LAW IN THE DIGITAL AGE – 2ND EDITION
by Allen Bargfrede
00148196 Book.................................... $19.99

MUSIC MARKETING
by Mike King
50449588 Book................................... $24.99

PROJECT MANAGEMENT FOR MUSICIANS
by Jonathan Feist
50449659 Book................................... $27.99

THE SELF-PROMOTING MUSICIAN – 3RD EDITION
by Peter Spellman
00119607 Book................................... $24.99

MUSIC PRODUCTION & ENGINEERING

AUDIO MASTERING
by Jonathan Wyner
50449581 Book/CD............................. $29.99

AUDIO POST PRODUCTION
by Mark Cross
50449627 Book................................... $19.99

THE SINGER-SONGWRITER'S GUIDE TO RECORDING IN THE HOME STUDIO
by Shane Adams
00148211 Book $16.99

UNDERSTANDING AUDIO – 2ND EDITION
by Daniel M. Thompson
00148197 Book................................... $24.99

SONGWRITING, COMPOSING, ARRANGING

ARRANGING FOR HORNS
by Jerry Gates
00121625 Book/Online Audio............ $19.99

BEGINNING SONGWRITING
by Andrea Stolpe with Jan Stolpe
00138503 Book/Online Audio $19.99

BERKLEE CONTEMPORARY MUSIC NOTATION
by Jonathan Feist
00202547 Book................................... $17.99

COMPLETE GUIDE TO FILM SCORING – 2ND ED.
by Richard Davis
50449607 .... $29.99

CONTEMPORARY COUNTERPOINT: THEORY & APPLICATION
by Beth Denisch
00147050 Book/Online Audio......... $22.99

THE CRAFT OF SONGWRITING
by Scarlet Keys
00159283 Book/Online Audio........... $19.99

JAZZ COMPOSITION
by Ted Pease
50448000 Book/Online Audio $39.99

MELODY IN SONGWRITING
by Jack Perricone
50449419 Book.................................... $24.99

MODERN JAZZ VOICINGS
by Ted Pease and Ken Pullig
50449485 Book/Online Audio $24.99

MUSIC COMPOSITION FOR FILM AND TELEVISION
by Lalo Schifrin
50449604 Book $34.99

MUSIC NOTATION
Preparing Scores and Parts
by Matthew Nicholl and Richard Grudzinski
50449540 Book................................... $16.99

MUSIC NOTATION
Theory and Technique for Music Notation
by Mark McGrain
50449399 Book................................... $24.95

POPULAR LYRIC WRITING
by Andrea Stolpe
50449553 Book.................................... $15.99

SONGWRITING: ESSENTIAL GUIDE
Lyric and Form Structure
by Pat Pattison
50481582 Book................................... $16.99
Rhyming
by Pat Pattison
00124366 2nd Ed. Book $17.99

SONGWRITING IN PRACTICE
by Mark Simos
00244545 Book................................... $16.99

SONGWRITING STRATEGIES
by Mark Simos
50449621 Book................................... $24.99

THE SONGWRITER'S WORKSHOP
Harmony
by Jimmy Kachulis
50449519 Book/Online Audio $29.99
Melody
by Jimmy Kachulis
50449518 Book/Online Audio $24.99